PASSPORT FRAUD: AN INTERNATIONAL VULNERABILITY

HEARING

BEFORE THE

SUBCOMMITTEE ON BORDER AND MARITIME SECURITY

OF THE

COMMITTEE ON HOMELAND SECURITY

HOUSE OF REPRESENTATIVES

ONE HUNDRED THIRTEENTH CONGRESS

SECOND SESSION

APRIL 4, 2014

Serial No. 113–62

Printed for the use of the Committee on Homeland Security

Available via the World Wide Web: http://www.gpo.gov/fdsys/

U.S. GOVERNMENT PRINTING OFFICE

88–781 PDF   WASHINGTON : 2014

For sale by the Superintendent of Documents, U.S. Government Printing Office
Internet: bookstore.gpo.gov   Phone: toll free (866) 512–1800; DC area (202) 512–1800
Fax: (202) 512–2250   Mail: Stop SSOP, Washington, DC 20402–0001

COMMITTEE ON HOMELAND SECURITY

MICHAEL T. McCAUL, Texas, *Chairman*

LAMAR SMITH, Texas
PETER T. KING, New York
MIKE ROGERS, Alabama
PAUL C. BROUN, Georgia
CANDICE S. MILLER, Michigan, *Vice Chair*
PATRICK MEEHAN, Pennsylvania
JEFF DUNCAN, South Carolina
TOM MARINO, Pennsylvania
JASON CHAFFETZ, Utah
STEVEN M. PALAZZO, Mississippi
LOU BARLETTA, Pennsylvania
RICHARD HUDSON, North Carolina
STEVE DAINES, Montana
SUSAN W. BROOKS, Indiana
SCOTT PERRY, Pennsylvania
MARK SANFORD, South Carolina
VACANCY

BENNIE G. THOMPSON, Mississippi
LORETTA SANCHEZ, California
SHEILA JACKSON LEE, Texas
YVETTE D. CLARKE, New York
BRIAN HIGGINS, New York
CEDRIC L. RICHMOND, Louisiana
WILLIAM R. KEATING, Massachusetts
RON BARBER, Arizona
DONDALD M. PAYNE, JR., New Jersey
BETO O'ROURKE, Texas
FILEMON VELA, Texas
ERIC SWALWELL, California
VACANCY
VACANCY

BRENDAN P. SHIELDS, *Staff Director*
MICHAEL GEFFROY, *Deputy Staff Director/Chief Counsel*
MICHAEL S. TWINCHEK, *Chief Clerk*
I. LANIER AVANT, *Minority Staff Director*

———

SUBCOMMITTEE ON BORDER AND MARITIME SECURITY

CANDICE S. MILLER, Michigan, *Chairwoman*

JEFF DUNCAN, South Carolina
TOM MARINO, Pennsylvania
STEVEN M. PALAZZO, Mississippi
LOU BARLETTA, Pennsylvania
VACANCY
MICHAEL T. McCAUL, Texas *(Ex Officio)*

SHEILA JACKSON LEE, Texas
LORETTA SANCHEZ, California
BETO O'ROURKE, Texas
VACANCY
BENNIE G. THOMPSON, Mississippi *(Ex Officio)*

PAUL L. ANSTINE, II, *Subcommittee Staff Director*
DEBORAH JORDAN, *Subcommittee Clerk*
ALISON NORTHROP, *Minority Subcommittee Staff Director*

CONTENTS

PASSPORT FRAUD: AN INTERNATIONAL VULNERABILITY

Friday, April 4, 2014

U.S. HOUSE OF REPRESENTATIVES,
SUBCOMMITTEE ON BORDER AND MARITIME SECURITY,
COMMITTEE ON HOMELAND SECURITY,
Washington, DC.

The subcommittee met, pursuant to call, at 9:02 a.m., in Room 311, Cannon House Office Building, Hon. Candice S. Miller [Chairwoman of the subcommittee] presiding.

Present: Representatives Palazzo, Jackson Lee, O'Rourke.

Also present: Representative Swalwell.

Mrs. MILLER. The Committee on Homeland Security, Subcommittee on Border and Maritime Security, will come to order.

This subcommittee is meeting today to examine the issue of passport security.

We are certainly pleased to be joined by Mr. Alan Bersin, who has been with this committee in the past, and we certainly appreciate his attendance here today. He is the assistant secretary for international affairs at the Department of Homeland Security.

Mr. John Wagner, who has also been before this subcommittee before. We appreciate his attendance today. He is the deputy assistant commissioner at U.S. Customs and Border Protection.

Ms. Brenda Sprague, who is the deputy assistant secretary for passport services at the Department of State.

Mr. Shawn Bray, who is the director of INTERPOL Washington, United States National Central Bureau.

I will more formally introduce them in just a moment. But let me recognize myself for an opening statement here this morning.

First of all, of course, let me start by saying, all of us, our thoughts and prayers are with the families of those killed and wounded at Fort Hood. This is a terrible, terrible incident that happened in my Ranking Member's State of Texas.

Certainly, as we begin the very difficult task of finding what went wrong there, we have to be mindful to support the men and women who wear the uniform not only when overseas, but certainly when they return home here as well.

This morning we are going to be talking about travel document security, which is a cornerstone of the United States effort to secure our homeland. It is integral to pushing our borders out.

The ability of terrorists and others who would seek to do us harm hinges, in large part, on the ability to travel, and if you make it hard for terrorists to cross our borders without being detected, future acts of terrorism hopefully can be prevented.

(1)

I want to begin by commending the Department of Homeland Security and the Department of State for the great progress made as we have strengthened the so-called outer ring of border security.

Today we conduct more vigorous vetting earlier in the process. We station DHS personnel in high-risk countries to prevent persons of concern from boarding the plane or getting a visa, and we are using biometrics to detect visa fraud.

In the past 3 years, this subcommittee has actually held six various hearings on visa and document security because we certainly understand the importance of 9/11 Commission's recommendations, and one of their conclusions, actually, as they said in that report, is that, for terrorists, travel documents are as important as weapons.

Vulnerabilities in our document security can be exploited by those who would do us harm. So we must have robust measures in place to deter and to ultimately detect those traveling on false documents.

To that end, we were certainly dismayed to learn from press reports that two of the passengers on the Malaysian Flight 370 boarded the aircraft using stolen passports.

While, of course, as has been reported, we don't have any reason to believe that these individuals were involved in an act of terrorism, it certainly highlights the vulnerability in the aviation systems abroad.

Our hearts, of course, and thoughts and prayers go out to the families who are still waiting to learn what has happened to their loved ones, and we certainly hope and pray that that plane will soon be found.

In the United States, through the work of the Department of Homeland Security, we have made the necessary changes to keep the flying public secure, and the ability of passengers to board a flight bound for the United States with a known lost or stolen passport is very, very low.

In the years after 2001, the international community, through INTERPOL, created a lost and stolen travel document database that gives countries a mechanism to both send the information to a central depository and to check against that database to make sure no one could enter a country or board a plane with a known lost or stolen passport.

Unfortunately, only three countries in the world routinely check flight manifests against that database: The United States, of course; the United Kingdom; and the United Arab Emirates.

So there is no question that more countries should follow our lead. Otherwise, international travelers, including Americans who travel internationally, are at risk.

According to INTERPOL, in 2013, travelers boarded international flights more than a billion times without having their passport numbers checked against the database.

Tools are in place to easily determine if a passport has been reported missing, and we should use every avenue at our disposal to encourage countries to do the right thing, including offering technical assistance where appropriate.

In addition to not consistently checking the lost and stolen passport database, most countries are also not consistently sharing lost and stolen passport information with the INTERPOL database.

The overwhelming majority of the 40 million records in the lost or stolen database comes from Visa Waiver Program countries in large part because it is conditioned for visa-free travel to the United States.

However, those countries do not routinely check their flight manifests against the database and, as a result, I will be introducing legislation and legislative solutions to encourage countries within the Visa Waiver Program to do so.

Because without timely reporting of lost and stolen travel documents, it becomes very difficult for CBP, through their advanced targeting system, to determine if someone is flying on a false document before they present themselves to a Customs Officer at an airport.

If a terrorist is intent to hijack an airplane, it might be too late. Even though the United States has a robust screening and vetting process for travelers, it doesn't mean that our work in this area is done.

I understand that CBP just recently began to check passengers on out-bound flights against the lost and stolen database, and we certainly are interested in hearing from our witnesses today why that wasn't done before.

Finally, I want to get an update on the work that the Department of Homeland Security and CBP and the State Department and INTERPOL have done since 9/11 to prevent those with lost, stolen, and fraudulent passports from getting on a plane bound for the United States.

While Americans should be confident that DHS is doing good work vetting all of the appropriate databases, we can and should work with our international partners to strengthen aviation security for Americans who travel abroad. This subcommittee stands ready to assist in any way that we can.

The Chairwoman would now recognize my Ranking Member on the subcommittee, the gentlelady from Texas, Ms. Jackson Lee, for her opening statement.

Ms. JACKSON LEE. Thank you very much, Madam Chairwoman. Good morning to the witnesses. Thank you so very much for your presence here today.

Thank you again, Madam Chairwoman, for reminding us, as I intended to do, of the tragedy that occurred in my home State, my neighbors at Fort Hood, Texas, and to again offer to those men and women who have been brave enough to put on the Nation's uniform to fight in far-away places our deepest concern and sympathy, certainly for the families who have lost their loved ones who, as I indicated, are willing to serve in the United States military and certainly those who are injured.

This is the second time that this tragedy occurred at Fort Hood and the second time that we have had to embrace those who, as I said, are our neighbors. I mourned with them in 2009 and will continue to do so now.

I hope this committee will have an opportunity to address the question of protecting, even as this is a military issue—protecting our men and women while they are on domestic soil and view it as a cause for zero tolerance for these kinds of incidences on the Nation's domestic military bases.

Again, my sympathy to not only the men and women at Fort Hood and the leadership, but also to the people of the State of Texas.

This is another tragedy that we are facing and trying to find solutions, and I would make mention that, even as this has gone into many, many days, that we still express our concern for the families of the passengers of Malaysia Airlines Flight 370. I hope that it will not be their final end that there has been no determination as to what occurred to that particular flight.

But today I am appreciative that we are holding this hearing, as I spoke to the Chairwoman in the immediacy of the hours of determining that there were passengers on that flight that had fraudulent passports.

Certainly there have been continuing investigations, and whether or not we have concluded that there was no connection, we do know that passengers traveled with fraudulent passports and as well that American citizens were on that flight.

While many questions remain unanswered regarding the tragic disappearance of Flight 370, we do not know, as I indicated, what connection those two passengers may have had to its demise, if any.

Two Iranian nationals were allowed to travel using Italian and Austrian passports that had been entered into INTERPOL's Stolen and Lost Travel Document database in 2012 and 2013.

Reports suggest that these individuals were not criminals or terrorists, but, rather, asylum seekers hoping to reach Europe.

Nevertheless, the fact that at least in certain countries travelers can readily board aircraft using passports that do not belong to them is a cause for concern. If a couple of asylum seekers can do it, so can terrorists or criminals.

After 9/11 and even in other countries before that, we know that we live in a different territory with different actors and different reasons for their actions. In fact, there are known examples of terrorists traveling on fraudulent documents.

According to INTERPOL, Ramzi Yousef, convicted of masterminding the 1993 World Trade Center bombing in New York, committed his crimes after traveling internationally on a stolen passport.

Also, Samantha Lewthwaite, the so-called "White Widow" of a London July 2005 suicide bomber, is wanted in Kenya and currently at large with aliases linked to a fraudulent passport and a passport reported stolen—evidence that this is a problem.

It is my understanding that the United States is ahead of most of the rest of the world when it comes to preventing individuals from traveling on lost, stolen, or fraudulent documents.

The Department of Homeland Security systematically checks all travelers' documents against appropriate lost and stolen databases. These checks yield results.

For example, in fiscal year 2013, U.S. Customs and Border Protection, CBP, reviewed 17,710 possible hits against lost and stolen databases, resulting in 496 individuals being denied from boarding planes to the United States. Already in fiscal year 2014 CBP has reviewed 10,806 possible hits, resulting in 159 individuals being denied boarding.

I also want to thank Homeland Security and the various agencies relevant to the issue of our border security for the extended perimeters and the improved security that we have had post-9/11.

We are clearly, as I have often said, in a better place than we were. We thank them again for their service and what we have been able to benefit from.

Since the Flight 370 incident, DHS has expanded its checks to include not just arriving passengers, but, also, those departing this country. While overdue, this step should close a remaining loophole regarding travelers using fraudulent documents to fly to or from this country.

I hope to hear from our DHS witnesses today about why departing passengers had not previously been included in their checks and whether any analysis had been done subsequently to determine whether passengers had been departing the United States on documents that do not belong to them.

I also hope that we will be able to embrace and include the airline industry as we move forward on a number of ways to ensure the safety and security of the traveling public.

I hope to hear from all of our witnesses about how we can encourage our international partners to follow the lead of the United States and a handful of other countries that regularly check travel documents against INTERPOL's SLTD database.

It is my understanding that traveling on lost, stolen, or otherwise fraudulent travel documents is already commonplace in certain parts of the world. Doing so is made possible because fewer than 20 of INTERPOL's 190 countries systematically check passports against SLTD.

Although the Flight 370 incident has focused attention on the vulnerability, it was already known to INTERPOL. In fact, speaking at the seventh Annual ID WORLD Summit in February just before flight the Flight 370 incident, INTERPOL Secretary General Ronald K. Noble lamented that only a handful of countries are systematically using SLTD to screen travelers when that technology and device is available, leaving our global security apparatus vulnerable to exploitation by criminals and terrorists.

The world is getting smaller. We travel from all over the world to all over the world. This is simply unacceptable.

I hope to hear from our witnesses today about how we can encourage other countries, particularly those we work closely with on aviation security matters, to begin regularly screening passenger documents against INTERPOL's database.

It is in that vein that I will be looking to draft legislation dealing with the enforcement aspect of this particular aspect of aviation travel.

The security of the traveling public, including U.S. citizens, traveling between foreign countries could well be at stake, as well as those traveling from foreign countries to the United States, as well as Americans leaving our soil and traveling elsewhere around the world.

Again, I thank Chairwoman Miller for holding today's hearing and the witnesses for joining us.

At this time I ask unanimous consent to allow Mr. Swalwell, a Member of the full committee, to sit and question the witnesses at today's hearing.

Mrs. MILLER. Without objection.

Ms. JACKSON LEE. I acknowledge Mr. O'Rourke as being present at the hearing today.

I yield back, Madam Chairwoman.

[The statement of Ranking Member Jackson Lee follows:]

STATEMENT OF RANKING MEMBER SHEILA JACKSON LEE

APRIL 4, 2014

Good morning. At the outset, I would like to say that my thoughts and prayers are with the passengers of Malaysia Airlines Flight 370 and their loved ones.

I would like to thank Chairwoman Miller for holding today's hearing to discuss security concerns regarding individuals traveling on lost, stolen, or fraudulent passports.

While many questions remain unanswered regarding the tragic disappearance of Flight 370, we do know that two passengers on that flight boarded the aircraft using stolen passports. Two Iranian nationals were allowed to travel using Italian and Austrian passports that had been entered into INTERPOL's Stolen and Lost Travel Document (SLTD) database in 2012 and 2013. Reports suggest that these individuals were not criminals or terrorists, but rather asylum seekers hoping to reach Europe.

Nevertheless, the fact that at least in certain countries travelers can readily board aircraft using passports that do not belong to them is cause for serious concern. If a couple of asylum seekers can do it, so can terrorists or criminals. In fact, there are known examples of terrorists traveling on fraudulent documents.

According to INTERPOL, Ramzi Yousef, convicted of masterminding the 1993 World Trade Center bombing in New York, committed his crimes after traveling internationally on a stolen passport. Also, Samantha Lewthwaite, the so-called "White Widow" of a London July 2005 suicide bomber, is wanted in Kenya and currently at large with aliases linked to a fraudulent passport and a passport reported stolen.

It is my understanding that the United States is ahead of most of the rest of the world when it comes to preventing individuals from traveling on lost, stolen, or fraudulent documents. The Department of Homeland Security (DHS) systematically checks all travelers' documents against appropriate lost and stolen databases. These checks yield results.

For example, in fiscal year 2013, U.S. Customs and Border Protection (CBP) reviewed 17,710 possible hits against lost and stolen databases, resulting in 496 individuals being denied from boarding planes to the United States. Already in fiscal year 2014, CBP has reviewed 10,806 possible hits, resulting in 159 individuals being denied boarding.

Since the Flight 370 incident, DHS has expanded its checks to include not just arriving passengers, but also those departing this country. While overdue, this step should close a remaining loophole regarding travelers using fraudulent documents to fly to or from this country.

I hope to hear from our DHS witnesses today about why departing passengers had not previously been included in their checks, and whether any analysis has been done subsequently to determine whether passengers had been departing the United States on documents that do not belong to them.

I hope to hear from all of our witnesses about how we can encourage our international partners to follow the lead of the United States and a handful of other countries that regularly check travel documents against INTERPOL's SLTD database.

It is my understanding that traveling on lost, stolen, or otherwise fraudulent travel documents is relatively commonplace in certain parts of the world. Doing so is made possible because fewer than 20 of INTERPOL's 190 countries systematically check passports against the SLTD. Although the Flight 370 incident has focused attention on this vulnerability, it was already known to INTERPOL.

In fact, speaking at the seventh Annual ID WORLD Summit in February, just before the Flight 370 incident, INTERPOL Secretary General Ronald K. Noble lamented that only a handful of countries are systematically using SLTD to screen travelers, leaving our global security apparatus vulnerable to exploitation by criminals and terrorists. This is unacceptable.

I hope to hear from our witnesses today about how we can encourage other countries, particularly those we work closely with on aviation security matters, to begin regularly screening passengers' documents against INTERPOL's database. The security of the traveling public, including U.S. citizens traveling between foreign countries, could well be at stake. Again, I thank Chairwoman Miller for holding today's hearing and the witnesses for joining us.

I yield back.

Mrs. MILLER. I thank the gentlelady.

Other Members of the committee are reminded that opening statements might be submitted for the record.

We are pleased today to have, as I mentioned, four very distinguished witnesses joining us today.

Ms. JACKSON LEE. Madam Chairwoman, would you just allow me to indicate that I am called to be part of a quorum in a markup and I will be away for just a moment. I thank the Chairwoman for her courtesy.

Mrs. MILLER. Certainly.

It is a busy morning here on the Hill and we are going to be having votes a little after 10:00. So we will move along here.

Mr. Alan Bersin is the assistant secretary of international affairs and chief diplomatic officer for the Department of Homeland Security. Previously, Mr. Bersin served as commissioner for the U.S. Customs and Border Protection.

Mr. John Wagner is the acting deputy assistant commissioner for the office of field operations in U.S. Customs and Border Protection. Mr. Wagner formerly served as executive director of admissibility and passenger programs with responsibility for all traveler admissibility-related policies and programs.

Ms. Brenda Sprague serves as deputy assistant secretary of state for passport services in the Bureau of Consular Affairs, a position she has held since July 2008. In this capacity, Ms. Sprague oversees a network of 28 agencies and centers that are responsible for the acceptance, adjudication, and issuance of U.S. passports.

Mr. Shawn Bray is the director of INTERPOL Washington, the United States National Central Bureau, a position he has held since 2012. As director, Mr. Bray acts on behalf of the attorney general as the official U.S. representative to INTERPOL. Mr. Bray has been focused on improving partnerships between the other 189 INTERPOL member countries and their U.S. Federal, State, local, and Tribal law enforcement counterparts.

The full statements of all of the witnesses will appear in the record.

The Chairwoman now recognizes Mr. Bersin for his statement.

STATEMENT OF ALAN D. BERSIN, ASSISTANT SECRETARY OF INTERNATIONAL AFFAIRS AND CHIEF DIPLOMATIC OFFICER, U.S. DEPARTMENT OF HOMELAND SECURITY

Mr. BERSIN. Thank you, Madam Chairwoman, Mrs. Miller, Congressmen O'Rourke and Swalwell. I appreciate this opportunity on this subject.

The International Criminal Police Organization, or INTERPOL, is the world's largest transnational police association with 190 member countries today. Each member country has a National

Central Bureau to conduct INTERPOL activities and coordinated services within its national territory.

Among the services INTERPOL provides to the law enforcement entities of every member country is access to its SLTD, Stolen and Lost Travel Document database. This database contains over 40 million records provided by nearly 170 of the organizations' members.

On March 9, INTERPOL confirmed that two of the passports used by passengers to board Malaysia Airlines Flight 370 had been recorded in its Stolen and Lost Travel Document database.

As noted by the Ranking Member, INTERPOL's Secretary General Ron Nobel noted, to the surprise of many, that very few countries systematically query the SLTD database for the purpose of verifying whether a passport has been reported as lost and stolen.

Even more troubling is the minuscule rate at which countries outside of Europe, Canada, and the United States visa-waiver countries are contributing information to the database.

Madam Chairwoman, as you noted, since 9/11, the United States Government and the American people have addressed the security vulnerabilities exposed so tragically on that day.

In the 12 years since, in a thoroughly bipartisan fashion in which this committee has played a significant role, we have together constructed a multi-layer, fully-automated interagency approach to homeland security.

As additional vulnerabilities have been revealed and are revealed, we examine and respond to them appropriately in concert with the Congress, as we do so today in the context of lost and stolen passports.

When an individual seeking admission to the United States presents a foreign passport, whether he or she seeks admission by land, by commercial air or by sea, that passport is screened against the SLTD database prior to admission, in fact, in many cases on multiple occasions. Now, as Mr. Wagner will explain, we also screen out-bound passports in the same way.

Unfortunately, most countries in the INTERPOL community do not screen travelers against the database as thoroughly as we do in the United States. Many, not at all.

More disturbing is the alarming number of countries that report very few and, in some cases, no lost or stolen passport data to the SLTD database. As a condition for participation, as the Chairwoman noted, visa waiver countries are required to do so.

The United States, Canada, and Europe, as well as the other VWP partners, accordingly have provided the vast majority of the 40 million records in the SLTD database.

Some of the most populous countries in the world, notably including China, India, and Indonesia, have contributed few, if any, records to the database.

Despite the remarkable development of the database, 40 million records added in the past 12 years, the lack of data provided by many INTERPOL member countries remains significant.

I have had the honor of serving on the INTERPOL executive committee and as vice president for the Americas since November 2012, and I have been urging the organization to prioritize the

SLTD program and other border security efforts as core functions of INTERPOL.

To be sure, Madam Chairwoman, Congressmen, there are real and current challenges to this vision. Despite the fact that DHS and the United States National Central Bureau have worked to incorporate recommendations for data reporting and response times into INTERPOL's standard operating procedures, many countries have not been able to connect their agencies and INTERPOL does not require them to do so.

The task ahead is encouraging our partners to more fully utilize the SLTD database and to engage in these kinds of border screening and security efforts. This can only add to its value from the standpoint of American security.

I look forward to exploring with you how we may best approach this latest challenge. It will not be the last, Madam Chairwoman and Congressmen, but I take from our past experience that we can forge and resolve this matter in a satisfactory cost-effective way.

Thank you for this opportunity again, and I look forward to responding to your questions.

[The joint prepared statement of Mr. Bersin and Mr. Wagner follows:]

JOINT PREPARED STATEMENT OF ALAN D. BERSIN AND JOHN P. WAGNER

APRIL 4, 2014

INTRODUCTION

Chairwoman Miller, Ranking Member Jackson Lee, and distinguished Members of the subcommittee. Thank you for holding this important hearing today to discuss document security in the context of international air travel.

On March 9, the International Criminal Police Organization (INTERPOL) confirmed that two of the passports used by passengers to board Malaysia Airlines Flight 370 had been recorded in its Stolen and Lost Travel Documents (SLTD) database. INTERPOL's Secretary General, Ron Noble, noted that very few countries systematically query the SLTD database for the purposes of verifying whether a passport has been reported as lost or stolen. INTERPOL has said that in 2013 travelers boarded flights more than a billion times without having their passport numbers checked against the SLTD database. This number does not include any flight to the United States, but it is striking nonetheless. Even more troubling is the poor rate at which countries outside the U.S. Visa Waiver Program (VWP) are contributing information on lost and stolen passports to the SLTD database.

At the moment, our thoughts and prayers are with the missing passengers and crew who were on Malaysia Airlines Flight 370. DHS appreciates the opportunity to discuss the important steps that we—in coordination with our partners at the Department of State and the U.S. National Central Bureau (USNCB)—have taken to mitigate vulnerabilities associated with persons attempting to travel on lost or stolen passports, which has been highlighted by the recent tragedy, and to talk about the importance of information exchange to the homeland security enterprise.

THE STOLEN AND LOST TRAVEL DOCUMENT DATABASE

INTERPOL is the world's largest international police organization with 190 member countries today. INTERPOL's primary goal is to ensure that police around the world have access to the tools and services necessary to do their jobs effectively. Among the services INTERPOL provides to the law enforcement entities of every member country is access to the SLTD database. The SLTD database is maintained by INTERPOL, and it contains over 40 million records provided by nearly 170 of the organization's members.

It is important to note that when an individual seeking admission to the United States, presents a passport, whether by land from Canada or Mexico, by commercial air, or by sea on a cruise ship, that passport is screened against the SLTD database prior to admission—in fact in many cases, they are screened against the database on multiple occasions. Unfortunately, most countries in the INTERPOL community do not screen travelers against the SLTD database as thoroughly as we do in the United States. The ability to screen travel information in advance—be it against the SLTD database or a national watchlist that included, for example, terrorist information—is an important element of effective border and transportation security.

More disturbing is the alarming number of countries that report very little—and in some cases no—lost and stolen passport data to INTERPOL for inclusion in the SLTD database. As a condition for participation, VWP countries are required to provide lost and stolen passport data to INTERPOL for inclusion in the SLTD database or to make such data available to the United States through other means as designated by the Secretary, and DHS continuously monitors that data to ensure compliance by our partners. The United States, Canada, and Europe, as well as our other VWP partners have provided the vast majority of the 40 million records in the SLTD database.

Alarmingly, some of the most populous countries in the world including China, India, and Indonesia, have contributed few—if any—records to the SLTD database. Despite the incredible development of the SLTD database since its inception following the September 11 attacks—40 million records added in the past 12 years is a truly noteworthy accomplishment—the lack of data provided by many INTERPOL member countries remains significant.

We firmly believe, based on DHS's operational experience since 9/11, that the automated and depersonalized screening of traveler data against derogatory administrative, counterterrorism, and law enforcement records is an essential part of the future for homeland security efforts around the world. The INTERPOL SLTD database is the quintessential example of one way countries can collaborate in preventing fraud and subsequent criminal activity. There is no reason why a passport should not be scanned every time an individual boards a plane to verify that the document provided is valid. These sorts of queries can be done almost instantaneously, occur completely automatically, and provide a first indicator of suspicion that can guide a law enforcement response in concert with the relevant passport issuing authority. The process provides significant confidence in the legitimacy of the document (assuming of course that the participating countries properly and accurately report their data into the SLTD database).

HOW THE UNITED STATES USES SLTD

U.S. Customs and Border Protection (CBP) uses the SLTD database and data from the Department of State's (DOS's) Consular Lost and Stolen Passport (CLASP) and the Consular Visa Lookout and Support System (CLASS) in the air, land, and sea environments to verify the validity of both U.S. and foreign passports. For VWP travelers, CBP vets all Electronic System for Travel Authorization applications against the SLTD database. In the land environment, when a traveler arrives at a land border port of entry, CBP officers will query the document in TECS,[1] which includes Lost and Stolen U.S. Passports and the INTERPOL SLTD for foreign passports. If CBP receives a hit, it refers the individual to secondary inspection for questioning. During the secondary inspection, CBP determines if the individual is a mala fide traveler or if the individual is the true bearer of the reported lost or stolen passport.

In the air and sea environments, when CBP receives inbound and outbound carrier advance passenger information system (APIS) data for travelers with a foreign passport, it queries the INTERPOL SLTD database for any matches to the document type—passport, number, and issuing country. For U.S. citizens utilizing U.S. passports, CBP queries TECS for matches to lost, stolen, and revoked U.S. Passports. In the air environment, if CBP detects lost, stolen, or revoked passports prior to boarding through CBP's pre-departure vetting or through the Immigration Advisory Program (IAP), CBP would make a recommendation to the air carrier not to board the passenger. If CBP notified the carrier, but the traveler was still allowed to board with the document that was the subject of a lost or stolen passport lookout, the carrier would be subject to a fine for violation of Section 273(a)(1) of the Immigration and Nationality Act.

---

[1] TECS (no longer an acronym) is a key border enforcement system supporting the vetting of travelers entering the United States and the requirements of other Federal agencies used for law enforcement and immigration benefit purposes. TECS supports the sharing of information about people who are inadmissible or may pose a threat to the security of the United States through the creation and query of "lookout records." TECS is used by more than 70,000 users, including users from more than 20 Federal agencies that use TECS in furtherance of their missions. TECS receives and processes traveler manifests from carriers and supports primary and secondary inspections for almost a million travelers and almost half a million vehicles at United States ports of entry each day.

CBP has also developed the Carrier Liaison Program (CLP), which enhances border security to the airlines and their security companies by identifying improperly documented passengers destined to the United States. CLP training enables participants, including airline check-in personnel, boarding agents, and security company staff, to receive hands-on instruction in fraudulent document identification, passenger assessment, impostor identification, and traveler document verification. When carriers encounter a lost or stolen travel document, CLP training instructs the carriers to contact CBP's Regional Carrier Liaison Groups (RCLGs). The RCLG offices are 24/7 operations maintained at the airports in New York, Miami, and Honolulu, with each RCLG maintaining responsibility for specific areas of the world to respond to carrier concerns. The RCLGs will respond in real-time to carrier inquiries concerning the validity of travel documented presented. After an RCLG determination of the lost/stolen travel document has been made, the RCLG will make a recommendation to board the passenger or to deny boarding. To date, the CLP has trained 33,600 airline and security personnel.

INTERPOL AND INFORMATION SHARING

The I–24/7 global police communications system, which our colleague Mr. Shawn Bray, the Director of the USNCB, can speak to at great length, is a marvel in today's world, and it is one that has largely gone unnoticed. Each of INTERPOL's 190 member countries has a National Central Bureau (NCB) that is typically housed within that country's National police agency. And most significantly, each of these NCBs is connected to the I–24/7 secure communications system. By using the INTERPOL network, the U.S. law enforcement community can exchange information in real time and in a secure manner with our police counterparts in every other INTERPOL member country around the world. This is an exceptional capability, and we have only begun to tap the potential it embodies.

To be sure, there are real and current challenges to this vision. Despite the fact that DHS and the USNCB have worked to incorporate recommendations for data reporting and response times into INTERPOL's approved SLTD standard operating procedures, INTERPOL does not require its member countries to implement them. With regard to screening passengers against the SLTD database, many countries do not have advance passenger information capabilities to screen travelers prior to arrival, or they have been unable to connect their immigration agencies to their NCBs in order to screen documents at the time of arrival. Many countries have been unable to connect their agencies that record lost or stolen passport information to their NCBs, so reporting that data has been a challenge. This may be due to a lack of the proper information technology systems within the country, internal restrictions on data sharing between agencies, or simple bureaucratic complexity (for example, some countries record lost identity documents at local police stations). These are all best practices that we employ here in the United States that we shall continue to encourage our partner countries to adopt.

To help address these challenges among its member countries, INTERPOL—with assistance from DHS—has recently established the Integrated Border Management Task Force (IBMTF). The IBMTF is charged with assisting member countries in their approach to border management, and how to utilize the tools and services INTERPOL offers to that end. The project has included, for example, trainings for immigration officials on using the SLTD database to screen in-bound passengers. The intent is to help member countries move toward more systematic approaches to the use of the SLTD database in daily operations. DHS remains supportive of INTERPOL's efforts in this regard.

INTERPOL understands, as we do at DHS, that sharing data on lost and stolen passports is an essential and fundamental part of protecting people against crime and terrorism. Whenever you are pulled over by State or local law enforcement, your driver's license is vetted to verify its validity and to determine any derogatory information for you. The SLTD database operates on the same principle, just on a global scale, and all countries should be encouraged to adopt similar measures. INTERPOL's SLTD database provides them with that opportunity. It is already built, already in use, and the United States has already proven it is a reliable repository for lost and stolen passport data that can effectively be used during border screening. The task ahead is encouraging our partners to more fully utilize it, which will in turn only further add to its value.

CONCLUSION

DHS has instituted procedures to vet all U.S. in-bound and out-bound international travelers against the SLTD database. Any person with a travel document that has been reported lost or stolen to INTERPOL, who attempts to board a plane to or from the United States, will be denied boarding until he can verify his identity.

The ability to screen for lost or stolen travel documents, however, hinges upon foreign countries reporting their data to INTERPOL. This is why DHS has invested significantly in ensuring that all VWP countries report lost and stolen passports to INTERPOL, since the SLTD database is only as valuable as the data it contains.

DHS's engagement strategy going forward is based on "Three P's": Populate, Process, and Promote. We will continue to ensure that all VWP countries populate the SLTD database effectively, and we will emphasize to our other foreign partners the critical importance of populating the SLTD database with their lost and stolen passport data. We will work closely with INTERPOL to ensure that effective processes exist to coordinate an appropriate law enforcement response when a lost or stolen passport is encountered. Lastly, we will work bilaterally and multilaterally to promote effective use of the SLTD database based on DHS's experiences. As the "Three P's" are implemented, DHS hopes to be even more effective in helping to secure the global aviation system, and U.S. citizens will have greater confidence in their safety abroad.

Thank you for the opportunity to testify today, for your continued support of the Department, and for your attention to this important issue. We would be pleased to answer any questions at this time.

Mrs. MILLER. Thank you very much, Mr. Bersin.

The Chairwoman now recognizes Mr. Wagner for his testimony.

STATEMENT OF JOHN P. WAGNER, ACTING DEPUTY ASSISTANT COMMISSIONER, OFFICE OF FIELD OPERATIONS, CUSTOMS AND BORDER PROTECTION, U.S. DEPARTMENT OF HOMELAND SECURITY

Mr. WAGNER. Chairman Miller, Ranking Member Jackson Lee, and distinguished Members of the committee, thank you for the opportunity to appear today and discuss the role of U.S. Customs and Border Protection in passport security.

I appreciate the opportunity to join my colleagues in speaking on this very important issue which supports the core mission of CBP.

Today I would like to discuss the sources of information available to CBP, how we query this information, as well as our operational responses in the different travel environments.

The ability for CBP officers to access real-time and reliable information on all travelers seeking admission to the United States is critical to our anti-terrorism and anti-fraud efforts.

However secure modern documents may be today, CBP must ensure that a traveler isn't fraudulently presenting another individual's valid passport or other travel documentation, whether the document is stolen or intentionally provided, to enter the United States.

CBP uses INTERPOL's Stolen and Lost Travel Document database, the SLTD, and Department of State's Consular Lost and Stolen Passport and Consular Lookout and Support Systems in the air, land, and sea environments to verify the validity and status of travel documents.

CBP also uses the SLTD data when a citizen of a Visa Waiver Program country applies for a travel authorization through the Electronic System for Travel Authorization, also known as ESTA. CBP has denied over 98,000 ESTAs since 2008 for lost and stolen records.

In all travel environments—air, land, and sea—CBP officers query travel documents against TECS, which is our primary database that includes access to many enforcement systems, including lost and stolen passport data, and against our automated targeting systems.

In the air and sea environment, CBP has the extra advantage of receiving airline traveler information prior to departure from the foreign location. This enables CBP to address potential risk factors and admissibility issues prior to boarding the aircraft.

CBP will coordinate through our National Targeting Center and our assets overseas in the Immigration Advisory Program or in preclearance or we may coordinate directly with the airline through our regional carrier liaison groups to prevent boarding in cases where the ESTA has been denied or if a traveler does not have a replacement document to the one reported lost or stolen. CBP has recommended over 650 no-board recommendations to carriers in the last 18 months.

In all environments, CBP coordinates with INTERPOL when matches to document queries are returned from the SLTD. Many of the cases are actually travelers with no mollified intent. They are simply travelers that have reported a lost document, but later found it and are trying now to use it for travel.

In this case, CBP will verify the person's identify and, if the passport is a U.S. passport, we will allow the traveler to proceed, but will seize the passport and return it to Department of State.

In other cases, the traveler will have a valid replacement document for the lost and stolen one and CBP will verify that they are the true bearer and allow the traveler to proceed. This often occurs in the air environment when the traveler has not updated their airline profile with an airline and the old passport data has been transmitted to us.

If the traveler is found to be presenting the lost or stolen passport as an imposter or has altered and tampered with the passport in any form, CBP will take appropriate law enforcement action against that traveler. In the last 18 months, CBP has seized over 300 lost and stolen documents used in an attempt to enter the United States fraudulently.

To enhance passport security operations, CBP has also developed the Carrier Liaison Program, which provides training to airlines and their security companies on identifying improperly documented passengers destined to the United States.

CLP training provides airline personnel hands-on instruction in fraudulent document identification, passenger assessment, imposter identification, and traveler document verification. To date, the CLP has trained 33,600 airline and security personnel.

When carriers encounter a lost or stolen document, CLP training instructs the carriers to contact CBP's regional carrier liaison groups that are 24/7 operations maintained at the airports in New York, Miami, and Honolulu.

The RCLGs will respond in real time to carrier inquiries concerning the validity of the travel document presented. After an RCLG determination of the lost and stolen travel document has been made, the RCLG will make the recommendation to board the passenger or deny boarding.

So in concert with our partners, CBP strives to ensure that travelers who present a risk are appropriately interviewed or vetted before boarding a flight bound for the United States and that any document deficiencies are addressed before traveling to the United States.

CBP has placed officers in strategic airports overseas to work with carriers and host nation authorities and has built strong liaisons with airline representatives to improve our ability to address threats as early as possible and effectively expand our security efforts beyond the physical borders of the United States.

These efforts seek to keep our transportation sector safe and prevent threats from ever reaching the United States. These efforts also enhance efficiency and create savings for the U.S. Government and the private sector by preventing inadmissible travelers from traveling to the United States.

Thank you for the opportunity to testify today, and I am happy to answer your questions.

Mrs. MILLER. Thank you very much, Mr. Wagner.

The Chairwoman now recognizes Ms. Sprague for her testimony.

STATEMENT OF BRENDA S. SPRAGUE, DEPUTY ASSISTANT SECRETARY FOR PASSPORT SERVICES, BUREAU OF CONSULAR AFFAIRS, U.S. DEPARTMENT OF STATE

Ms. SPRAGUE. Chairwoman Miller, distinguished Members of the committee, thank you for the opportunity to testify today about the many things the Department of State does to promote the security of the U.S. passport and deter passport fraud. I appreciate your focus on this important topic.

We at the Department of State believe, to prevent passport fraud, you need to focus on five areas: A sophisticated document with technically advanced security features; a robust and vigorous adjudication system; real-time sharing of data; a proactive anti-fraud program; and outreach to U.S. citizens to educate them about the important form of identification.

Because of the access the passport provides, we have spent years creating products with high-tech security features, including photo biometrics, secure laminates, microprinting, color-shifting ink, and enhanced electronics, that render these documents virtually impossible to counterfeit.

But as the sophistication of the U.S. passport increases, so do the efforts of those attempting to commit passport fraud. Today's passport fraud most often involves fraudulent birth certificates, fake identities, and look-alike photos.

Passport adjudicators spend hours annually in mandated training to make certain that they have the skills to identify various types of fraud. We also integrate several real-time front-end database checks into our adjudication system. But this is not enough.

As recent events have shown, even a well-designed, well-adjudicated passport is still a vulnerability in the wrong hands.

Domestically, we counter this by reporting lost, stolen, and revoked passports to TECS, the system Custom and Border Protection uses to screen arriving passengers at U.S. ports of entry.

In turn, CBP TECS sends us U.S. passports it seizes at U.S. borders so that we can identify patterns and determine whether the bearer submits a fraudulent passport application.

Internationally, we lead the way in reporting lost, stolen, and re-voked passport data to the INTERPOL Lost and Stolen Travel Documents.

We provide INTERPOL with real-time data, including the passport number and date of issue, so it is accessible to member law enforcement authorities world-wide.

We also require all countries in our Visa Waiver Program to report lost and stolen data to INTERPOL if they wish to maintain VWP status.

The Departments of State and Homeland Security use the SLTD to vet visa applicants, in-bound flight and vessel manifests, and people crossing land borders at all U.S. ports of entry.

If used consistently by international law and border enforcement agencies, the SLTD effectively prevents imposters from using lost and stolen passports they bought or obtained fraudulently for travel.

Though I believe our documents and systems are strong, there is never time to rest on our laurels. The U.S. passport is one of the most sought-after documents in the world.

Not only is it an international travel document, it is also a legal form of identification and might be used to determine eligibility for entitlement benefits, to apply for a driver's license, to confirm employment eligibility, to qualify for a mortgage, or to open a bank account.

This means that we must continually assess the passport security features and design for potential vulnerabilities and incorporate new measures as technology advances.

Through our website, travel.state.gov, and through community outreach by our 29 passport agencies, we remind U.S. citizens of the importance of safeguarding their passports and provide guidance for reporting to us if the documentation is lost or stolen.

We continually review our methods to improve our passport issuance system and fraud detection capabilities and look for new ways to partner with other agencies, educate the public and strengthen existing procedures.

We welcome opportunities to expand these efforts with Federal, State, local, and international agencies to protect our citizens and promote safe, secure, and legal travel throughout the world.

Thank you again for the opportunity to appear before you today. I am happy to answer any questions you may have.

[The prepared statement of Ms. Sprague follows:]

PREPARED STATEMENT OF BRENDA S. SPRAGUE

APRIL 4, 2014

Chairwoman Miller, Ranking Member Jackson Lee, thank you for the opportunity to testify today about the many things the Department of State does to promote security through interagency cooperation, international data sharing, and integrity of the U.S. passport.

First, I'd like to offer my thoughts and prayers to the family and loved ones of those on Malaysia Airlines Flight 370. Our heartfelt thanks go out to the international effort of men and women working around-the-clock to solve the mystery of this plane's disappearance.

The initial investigation uncovered a troubling case of imposters using stolen Austrian and Italian passports to board the Malaysian jetliner. Although it might not be related to the plane's ultimate fate, this episode underscores the importance of continued and comprehensive data sharing among the Federal and international communities to prevent acts of international terrorism, illegal immigration, and other serious forms of international crime, as well as theft or misuse of passports.

The State Department works closely with our colleagues at the Department of Homeland Security, the Department of Justice, and other agencies to ensure our documents, and reports of their misappropriation, are shared broadly and quickly.

Domestically, we do this through data sharing of U.S. lost, stolen, and revoked passport data to TECS, a system used by the U.S. Customs and Border Protection to screen arriving travelers at ports of entry. We also send to TECS information we receive about lost and stolen foreign passports.

Internationally, we have been in the forefront of a significant push to promote reporting of lost and stolen passport data to the INTERPOL Stolen and Lost Travel Document—or SLTD—database. The State Department provides INTERPOL with comprehensive, real-time data on lost, stolen, and revoked U.S. passports—including the passport number and date of issue—so it is accessible to member law enforcement authorities world-wide. Annually, about 300,000 U.S. passport books and 20,000 passport cards are reported by U.S. citizens as lost or stolen—resulting in more than 3.2 million reports to the SLTD database since we began participating in 2004. The Department chose to add revoked passport data to the SLTD in 2010, and since then, have reported more than 3,500 revoked passports.

The Departments of State and Homeland Security use SLTD to vet visa applicants, in-bound flight and vessel manifests, and land border crossers at U.S. ports of entry. U.S. Customs and Border Protection officers at U.S. ports of entry send to the Department seized U.S. passports which we analyze to look for patterns and determine whether the bearer submitted a fraudulent passport application. Applications that exhibit evidence of fraud, complicity in alien smuggling, or other derogatory information are then referred to Fraud Prevention Managers in the domestic passport agencies and centers, and Diplomatic Security field offices for further investigation and possible prosecution. Where warranted, this information might be input into internal systems to be used if the bearer of the passport applies for another passport.

On the international front, the State Department works with member countries of the Asia-Pacific Economic Cooperation (APEC) alliance to detect documents reported as lost or stolen. This program, called the Regional Movement Alert System—or RMAS—is geared toward preventing criminals from boarding flights to participating countries. We are also engaging Taiwan—a non-INTERPOL member—to provide direct two-way transmission of lost, stolen, and revoked U.S. and Taiwanese passport data.

Perhaps most importantly, U.S. law requires all 37 countries participating in the Visa Waiver Program (VWP), as well as Taiwan, to report lost and stolen passport data to the United States Government via INTERPOL or through other means designated by the Secretary of Homeland Security. We believe approximately 70 percent of the SLTD's current data comes from VWP countries. The Department of State cannot compel foreign countries to check against this database; however, the Department does automatically screen against the SLTD database—i.e., electronic applications of immigrant and nonimmigrant visa applicants are screened against the INTERPOL database to ensure they are not using a passport that was reported lost or stolen.

Despite the Department's important domestic and international efforts to track reports of lost, stolen, or revoked documents, challenges remain which must be addressed. That's why the State Department must have other fraud prevention tools to help us verify citizens' identity and entitlement to a U.S. passport.

The U.S. passport is one of the most sought-after documents in the world. Although primarily used for international travel, it is also a legal form of identification and might be used to verify eligibility for Social Security, health care, or entitlement benefits. It can also be used to apply for a driver's license, obtain a mortgage, and verify employment eligibility. A passport is also one of the few photo identification documents available to minors and can be used in support of school enrollment or educational assistance. These key points, along with the message of keeping the passport secure, are communicated to the public at outreach events, through the travel.state.gov website, and through social media tools.

Because of the access a passport provides, we have invested in high-tech security features including photo biometrics, secure laminates, micro-printing, color shifting security ink, and enhanced electronics that render these documents virtually impossible to counterfeit.

As the sophistication and complexity of the U.S. passport has increased, so have the efforts of those attempting to commit passport fraud. The days of carefully peeling back the cover to replace the photo in a U.S. passport are long past. Today's passport fraud most often involves fraudulent supporting identity ("breeder") documents: Fraudulent birth certificates, false identities, and look-alike photos (sometimes with the cooperation of the legitimate bearer), are a few of the methods employed by imposters and other criminals.

To counter breeder document and identity fraud, we employ a robust fraud prevention strategy that includes in-depth training to our adjudicators, verifying information against Government and commercial databases, and technology, such as facial recognition. Our employees receive twice-monthly training to identify various types of fraud and highlight current trends in this type of fraud. We also integrate several real-time, front-end database checks into our adjudication system including facial recognition, Social Security, and death record verifications.

During the adjudication process, we use the National Law Enforcement Telecommunications System network to verify drivers' licenses. We run checks against files from the FBI to identify people on probation, parole, or pre-trial release who might be trying to obtain a U.S. passport to flee the country. Additionally, we use the services of several commercial data providers which allow our employees to verify an applicant's social footprint and detect fraudulent addresses, phone numbers, and other discrepancies in their application information.

Though I believe our systems and processes are strong, none is ever invulnerable. That's why we continually review our methods to improve issuance and fraud detection and look for new ways to strengthen existing procedures.

In this vein, we are currently developing a system that will allow citizens to report lost and stolen passport books and passport cards on-line immediately, thereby speeding the information-sharing process. We chair an interagency working group that meets weekly developing a next generation passport product that might include—among other advanced features—laser-perforated pages to prevent page substitutions.

The Department engages actively with State vital records bureaus to encourage contributions to a National centralized database of birth and death records provided by The National Association for Public Health Statistics and Information Systems. We are implementing a Memorandum of Understanding with the Federal Bureau of Prisons, and engaging State corrections agencies to share parole and pre-trial data.

To protect our citizens and promote safe, secure, and legal travel throughout the world, we welcome opportunities to continue to expand these efforts with Federal, State, local, and international agencies.

Thank you again for the opportunity to appear before you today. I am happy to answer any questions you might have.

Mrs. MILLER. Thank you very much, Ms. Sprague.

The Chairwoman now recognizes Mr. Bray for his testimony.

STATEMENT OF SHAWN A. BRAY, DIRECTOR, INTERPOL WASHINGTON, U.S. NATIONAL CENTRAL BUREAU, U.S. DEPARTMENT OF JUSTICE

Mr. BRAY. Thank you, Chairwoman Miller, Ranking Member Jackson Lee, and distinguished Members of the subcommittee.

It is an honor to be here today to provide you with an interview of INTERPOL's Stolen and Lost Travel Documents database, or SLTD, and how INTERPOL Washington and our partner agencies utilize this global resource to combat transnational crime and terrorism.

Before I get started, I would like to echo the previous statements of the panel regarding the tragic disappearance of Malaysia Airlines Flight 370. At INTERPOL Washington, our thoughts and prayers remain with the families and loved ones of the flight's passengers and crew. This incident certainly serves to underscore the need for coordination and collaboration across international borders to create a safer, more secure world for us all.

As you are aware, the International Criminal Police Organization, commonly known as INTERPOL, is the largest police organization in the world. Its membership is comprised of the national police authorities from 190 member countries, all of which participate in the organization on a voluntary basis.

INTERPOL exists to ensure and promote the widest possible mutual assistance between these police authorities. In order to achieve this high level of cooperation, each INTERPOL member country is required to establish and maintain a National Central Bureau.

INTERPOL Washington is that National Central Bureau for the United States. A component of the Department of Justice, we are unique in that we are also co-managed by the Department of Homeland Security.

In our 46th year of operation, INTERPOL Washington is supported by a multi-sector workforce consisting of a full-time staff from the Department of Justice and additional senior personnel representing more than 30 U.S. law enforcement agencies.

Simply stated, our mission is to facilitate international police cooperation, communication, and investigations through INTERPOL on behalf of the United States.

We support and heavily utilize INTERPOL's databases and resources, its secure global police communications system, the I–24/7, in order to accomplish this mission.

It is the I–24/7 that connects the U.S. directly with INTERPOL, its resources, but, also, directly with our 189 other country member partners.

The use of its databases and I–24/7 are governed by INTERPOL's rules on the processing of data. It is these rules that allow INTERPOL Washington to extend the services and data, including the SLTD to U.S. law enforcement.

In accordance with our internal information-sharing strategy, INTERPOL Washington has now extended the ability to query SLTD to all Federal, State, local, and Tribal authorities through existing U.S. law enforcement data systems.

The SLTD itself is essentially a searchable repository of stolen and lost passport visa and identity document information designed to help prevent illicit international travel and false impersonation by criminals and terrorists.

A query against the SLTD database in which there is a match will result in the return of only information about the suspect document itself, but will not include personally identifiable information about the document holder.

Although strongly encouraged by INTERPOL, participation in SLTD is voluntary and does vary country by country. The United States has embraced SLTD in its efforts as a critical component of its border security and transportation strategies.

In the United States, the Bureau of Consular Affairs at the Department of State is our designated partner and source for the stolen and lost passport data that is populated into the Stolen and Lost Travel Documents database.

Currently, the United States maintains over 3 million of the more than 40 million records contained in the SLTD. U.S. participation in SLTD is managed at INTERPOL Washington by our operations and command center.

Working on a 24-by-7 basis, we coordinate the entry of that U.S. passport data into the SLTD and, also, verify and resolve any matches against the database by either foreign or domestic authorities.

In 2013, U.S. law enforcement, border security and consular authorities queried the SLTD more than 238 million times, accounting for approximately 30 percent of all query activity world-wide.

These queries resulted in more than 25,000 matches against the database, the overwhelming majority of which were resolved administratively.

A small number of these hits, however, represented a serious potentially criminal concern and were immediately referred to appropriate law enforcement authorities for further investigation.

As you can see, INTERPOL Washington has aggressively pursued the use of SLTD to enhance and support our National security and investigations.

We will also continue to explore additional applications for SLTD to further assist our law enforcement community and ensure the safety of the American people.

Chairwoman Miller, Ranking Member Jackson Lee, and distinguished Members of the subcommittee, I sincerely appreciate the opportunity to testify about our role in this important program, and I would be pleased to answer any questions you have at this time.

[The prepared statement of Mr. Bray follows:]

PREPARED STATEMENT OF SHAWN A. BRAY

APRIL 4, 2014

Chairwoman Miller, Ranking Member Jackson Lee, and distinguished Members of the subcommittee, it is an honor to be here today to provide you with an overview of the INTERPOL Stolen/Lost Travel Document Database, or SLTD, and how INTERPOL Washington, the United States National Central Bureau, and its partner agencies utilize this international resource to combat transnational crime and terrorism.

BACKGROUND

INTERPOL

The International Criminal Police Organization—INTERPOL—is the largest international police organization in the world. Its membership is comprised of the respective national police authorities of its 190 member countries, which participate on a voluntary basis.

INTERPOL is a world-renowned brand in the international law enforcement community, but one that is often misunderstood by the public at large. Simply put, INTERPOL exists to ensure and promote the widest possible mutual assistance between the criminal police authorities of its member countries, and it seeks to " . . . establish and develop all institutions likely to contribute effectively to the prevention and suppression of ordinary law crimes."[1] INTERPOL is both mindful of the differing national laws of its member countries and active in its protection of human rights.

INTERPOL National Central Bureaus

Under INTERPOL's constitution, each member country is required to establish and maintain a "National Central Bureau", or NCB, responsible for ensuring the "constant and active cooperation" of the particular country.[2] An NCB serves as a critical link between the national law enforcement authorities of an INTERPOL member country, its foreign counterparts, and the INTERPOL General Secretariat.[3] Except for certain general guidelines and conditions of membership in INTERPOL,

---

[1] Article 2, Constitution of the International Criminal Police Organization—INTERPOL.
[2] Ibid, Article 31.
[3] Ibid, Article 32.

the structure, placement, and operation of an NCB is entirely within the control and discretion of the respective member country.

INTERPOL Washington—The United States National Central Bureau

Located in Washington, DC, INTERPOL Washington is the United States' National Central Bureau (USNCB). Our agency is unique in that it is a component of the U.S. Department of Justice and co-managed with the Department of Homeland Security under a Memorandum of Understanding.[4] INTERPOL Washington's mission is well-defined by statute and regulation and includes facilitating international police cooperation; transmitting information of a criminal justice, humanitarian, and other law enforcement related nature, and coordinating and integrating information in international criminal investigations.[5] Staffed entirely by U.S. law enforcement agents, officers, and analysts, INTERPOL Washington provides the means for over 18,000 Federal, State, local, and Tribal law enforcement agencies in the United States to communicate and collaborate with police globally. Just to clarify any potential ambiguity, let me underscore that the USNCB is not a part of the INTERPOL organization. It is a U.S. Government agency that serves as the U.S. link to INTERPOL.

Sharing INTERPOL Information

Fundamental to INTERPOL are its core functions to provide its member countries with secure global police communication services and access to its operational data services and databases. This is achieved through an encrypted, virtual private network known as the "I–24/7" secure communications system. INTERPOL ensures the quality of its data and the efficiency with which it is processed by adhering to a transparent set of operating guidelines known as *INTERPOL's Rules on the Processing of Data,* or RPD.

Under the RPD, NCBs may directly access INTERPOL's Information System. This access permits an NCB to manage its data contained in the system; query INTERPOL's databases; transmit messages; obtain and use INTERPOL Notices, and follow up on positive database query results. The RPD also allows NCBs to extend system access to their respective national authorities. In the United States, INTERPOL Washington extends query access to INTERPOL's investigative databases, which includes the Stolen/Lost Travel Documents Database, or SLTD, to all U.S. law enforcement, border protection, and consular authorities in support of their official duties.

The Stolen/Lost Travel Document Database (SLTD)

Terrorist attacks over the last few decades gave rise to the realization that many of the perpetrators were known suspects who had been traveling internationally while concealing their identity through the use of false passports. To address this threat, INTERPOL conceived the idea of creating a technology that would allow the real-time verification of travel documents that had been reported lost, stolen, or revoked by their respective national issuing authorities.

Developed in 2000 as a database of blank passports that had been reported stolen, SLTD rapidly expanded to include travel documents reported as stolen from, or lost by, the bearer. Becoming fully operational in July 2002, SLTD has grown from housing less than 300,000 records to more than 40,000,000 records in 2014, searchable in real time via fixed or mobile network database solutions. Using either solution, query results are available to authorized law enforcement and border security users in mere seconds.

The SLTD is one of the largest INTERPOL databases and it is considered among the world's primary tools for detecting stolen and lost travel documents in order to prevent illicit international travel and false personation by criminals and terrorists. Specifically, SLTD is a searchable repository of non-personal information drawn from passports, visas, and identity documents that have been reported stolen or lost by issuing authorities of INTERPOL member countries. It also includes information about stolen passport blanks and travel documents that have been revoked by an issuing national authority.

SLTD-authorized users are able to query specific passport numbers against the database in support of investigative or border security functions. A positive "hit" against the database will return data elements about a suspect document that include the issuing country, document type, date of the theft or loss, and a limited

---

[4] Memorandum of Understanding Between the U.S. Department of Homeland Security and the U.S. Department of Justice Pertaining to U.S. Membership in the International Criminal Police Organization (INTERPOL), Management of the INTERPOL-U.S. National Central Bureau, and Related Matters.

[5] 22 U.S.C. 263a; Title 28 CFR Subpart F–2 § 0.34.

amount of information related to the circumstances of the theft or loss, as provided by the INTERPOL reporting country. SLTD data does not include Personally Identifiable Information about passport holders, as defined under U.S. law, nor does the database provide access to information about all U.S. passports—only those that have been reported as stolen, lost, or revoked by issuing national authorities.

Only a member country's passport issuing authority, in coordination with its corresponding NCB, is authorized to enter and modify records in SLTD pertaining to the theft, loss, or revocation of its national travel documents. In the United States, the Department of State's Bureau of Consular Affairs is the designated source for lost, stolen, or revoked U.S. passport data submitted to SLTD through INTERPOL Washington. Currently, more than 3 million of the more than 40 million records contained in SLTD pertain to U.S. passports.

Although strongly encouraged by INTERPOL, participation in SLTD is voluntary on the part of INTERPOL member countries. While levels of participation vary on a country-by-country basis, the United States has embraced SLTD as a critical part of its strategy to combat illicit international travel and enhanced border security.

United States Utilization of SLTD

United States participation in SLTD is managed through our Operations and Command Center. Working 24/7/365, INTERPOL Washington partners with U.S. Customs and Border Protection (CBP) and the Department of State to make SLTD available for vetting against all in-bound and out-bound international travelers and visa applicants. With respect to international air travel, CBP receives Advance Passenger Information System (APIS) data from the carriers for those travelers inbound to and out-bound from the United States. CBP queries the foreign travel document data it receives via APIS data against SLTD for any matches to the listed travel documents. As an additional security measure, INTERPOL Washington also makes available all INTERPOL Notices and lookouts for fugitives, persons of interest, missing persons, and career criminals to CBP and all U.S. law enforcement via DHS's TECS and the National Crime Information Center database administered by the FBI.

In the event of a hit, our command center staff immediately seeks to verify and resolve all matches against SLTD on foreign travel documents with our foreign partners. Conversely, command center staff also coordinates with our international counterparts to resolve cases involving matches on U.S. passports presented at foreign border control points and to coordinate the appropriate administrative or law enforcement action.

In 2013, U.S. law enforcement, border security, and consular authorities queried SLTD more than 238 million times through INTERPOL Washington, which accounted for approximately 30 percent of all queries conducted by authorities worldwide. Of the more than 25,000 hits against the database that occurred during that time, the overwhelming majority were resolved administratively. A small number of these hits, however, represented a serious, potentially criminal concern, and were referred to the appropriate law enforcement authority for further investigation and resolution.

For example, INTERPOL Madrid coordinated with INTERPOL Washington last year to prevent an imposter, a Gambian national using stolen or lost U.S. passport, from traveling to New York. Investigation revealed the passport had been issued less than 30 days earlier. The subject was denied entry to the United States and the passport was recovered by Spanish authorities for return to U.S. authorities. The matter was referred to Spanish authorities for further investigation.

In another example, INTERPOL Sofia intercepted an Iranian national, who was traveling on a stolen or lost U.S. passport and posing as a U.S. citizen. INTERPOL Washington coordinated with U.S. and Bulgarian authorities to determine the subject's true identity, which resulted in his arrest and the recovery of the passport.

In addition to the large-scale, systematic screening of international travelers, SLTD may also be queried in support of an investigation or other official matter. Building upon our *Law Enforcement Information Sharing Strategy,* we have now extended the ability to query SLTD to all local, State, Federal, and Tribal law enforcement agencies through nationally-available systems such as Nlets and N–DEx, the FBI's National Data Exchange.

Continuing Challenges

Notwithstanding the considerable progress that has been achieved since SLTD was first introduced, significant challenges remain in realizing its full potential. Of the INTERPOL member countries that participate in SLTD, many do not routinely contribute data on lost/stolen documents and fewer still regularly screen travel documents against the database. This participation varies on a country-by-country basis as a consequence of such factors as national policy, lack of connection or co-operation between law enforcement, issuing, and border control authorities, and capacity, i.e. cost of deployment and existing IT infrastructure.

The Way Forward

Just as the use of SLTD continues to grow, so too does INTERPOL's vision for detecting and deterring the illicit international travel of criminals and terrorists. Building upon I–24/7, its proven and highly adaptable global police communications network, INTERPOL is today implementing additional tools and services to assist law enforcement. Recently made operational, INTERPOL's TDAWN—Travel Documents Associated With Notices—enables law enforcement officers to identify wanted criminals that are subject to INTERPOL Notices when checking associated travel documents.

TDAWN, as well as other operational and forensic databases that now form the "INTERPOL Travel ID and Document Center", hold promise to further enhance efforts to combat the illicit international travel that threatens our public safety, transportation, commerce, and national security. And, just as INTERPOL Washington has aggressively exploited the use of SLTD, we will continue to explore the potential applications of these new and promising capabilities.

Chairman Miller, Ranking Member Jackson Lee, distinguished Members of the subcommittee; I sincerely appreciate the opportunity to testify about this important program and our role in it. I would be happy to answer any questions you may have.

Mrs. MILLER. Thank you very much.

I certainly appreciate all of the witnesses. You have been very, very informative on this, I think, very interesting issue and something that I think the United States Congress needs to be looking at a bit more.

Because, really, the purpose of this hearing—first of all, we have a great story to tell, as has been mentioned here this morning.

The United States has a great story to tell about how significantly we have ratcheted up our security—our document security, et cetera, for our American citizens, particularly flying domestically here since 9/11. It really is a remarkable achievement by our Nation, I think.

So I want to make sure that our United States citizens do recognize and have a high degree of confidence and comfort level in the fact of what is happening with our various Government agencies when our citizens are traveling domestically here.

But as we are very aware now—and I think the American citizens are much more aware because of the tragedy of Malaysian Flight 370—that, if you are an American citizen and you are traveling internationally, particularly from one international country to another, they don't have the same type of security with their data documentation that we do.

I suppose we know that, but, yet, we need to look at what types of things we could do, perhaps, to incentivize others to improve a bit, particularly when we see in the Malaysia Flight 370 there were American citizens traveling on that aircraft.

So, since that has happened, as the world continues to search for that flight, we decided to have this hearing this morning really to look into this issue a bit and explore what types of options we might have.

Certainly one that comes to mind immediately—and it has been mentioned here, of course, extensively in the testimony today and in our opening comments, both myself and my Ranking Member.

I mean, we have 38 countries—we have a list of the 38 countries that do—these are our friends. These are our allies, these nations—that are under the visa-free travel, the VWP program.

This is a program the United States started back in the 1980s, really, as a way to expedite travel from our allied countries into the United States for tourism, for commerce, et cetera.

Since 9/11, we have had great success with them certainly checking—or giving us information if there are lost or stolen passports. So that is all good.

However, it is interesting—and it really has come to light, I think, because of the Malaysia flight—that these same countries are not really checking as they could for the potential of stolen or lost passports on their database when people are getting on their flights.

So, again, these are other nations. I think the United States—obviously, they are our friends. They are our allies, et cetera. But we do have this particular program with them.

I am just wondering—as I mentioned in my opening statement, it is my intention—we are looking at introducing legislation that would require them, as a participant in this program, to really not only just regularly submit information on lost and stolen passports, but, really, for these countries also to routinely check the database for passengers who are boarding these flights.

I mean, you look at the list of the countries here. As I say, these are our friends and allies—our closest allies in the world, really. I mean, you look at France and Germany, Greece, Ireland, Italy, et cetera, and this information is available.

Really, in some ways, it would seem to me that many of these countries don't need to be incentivized by the United States. Perhaps they will start doing it on their own after what has come to light with the Malaysia flight.

But I guess I would throw that question out. Maybe start with Mr. Bersin.

What is your thought about actually legislation about something like that? What do you think would be the reaction of our allied countries for something like that? Would they consider it an intrusion? What would your thought be on something like that?

Mr. BERSIN. Madam Chairwoman, so, of course, you recognize that, pending the submission of legislation, this is a—in which the department would have a formal review process——

Mrs. MILLER. Right.

Mr. BERSIN [continuing]. This is a good-faith response to your inquiry based——

Mrs. MILLER. I appreciate that. Yes. There has not been legislation introduced. But, as I say, it is my intent to do so.

Mr. BERSIN. So looking at the way in which visa waiver countries operate now, we do require them to populate the database so that every time someone comes on the way to the United States we can query that database maintained by INTERPOL, operated, as Ms. Sprague indicated, by the NCB and find lost and stolen documents. The number is great because of the requirement.

Also, when you get on a foreign airline and they come to—someone is coming on a foreign airline from those countries, we get the same benefit because the advanced passenger information requirement pertains to any flight from any country, whether visa waiver or else, coming toward the United States.

The question you raised, which is whether, as a condition of participating in the Visa Waiver Program, they ought to be compelled to screen against the database with regard to all flights, regardless of whether they are coming toward us or going elsewhere, poses an interesting policy question.

It does address the issue that we see highlighted by Malaysia Airline Flight 370 and the two Iranians using the lost or stolen passport issued in Italy and Austria. It is a legitimate issue.

I believe, though, that we are going to have to assess whether, of all the things that we would require that do not have a direct impact on us—whether that would be one of them I think is an open question, speaking frankly. It is an important question, but I don't think that the answer is a straightforward "yes."

Thank you.

Mrs. MILLER. I appreciate that.

Anyone else have a comment on that?

Mr. Wagner.

Mr. WAGNER. We do encourage many nations to develop their own advanced passenger information systems, and we work with them to help them do that. You know, we try to put some consistency in the format and the data elements so the airlines don't have many different systems to provide to many different countries.

But it starts with collecting passenger manifest information at an appropriate time in the airline process so a government can take a response and, you know, a lot of countries don't have the capacity to even do that. Some of them do in varying degrees.

Then the ability to run that set of data against the different databases that are there, you know, for that government to access and—you know, it really becomes a technology and a resource issue for a lot of the governments to do.

In the cases where we have had some of our close partners develop these type systems, we have also brokered some arrangements to help them target that information and help them review it and exchange information in that, and we have located some of our personnel on the ground to work with their authorities to help them adjudicate a lot of those passenger manifests. We have officers in Panama. We have officers in Mexico. It is an extension of our Immigration Advisory Program.

But we can work with travelers traveling—we can work with those governments to identify travelers traveling into those countries to help them to identify that.

We have had some success with the use of lost and stolen documents entering Panama and entering Mexico to be able to do that. So we will continue to push certain countries to expand on those agreements and, really, on those capabilities.

Mrs. MILLER. Following up, Mr. Wagner, because it was in your testimony, I think—or one of you—that testified that CBP was going to be—it just started a screening for lost and stolen passports on the out-bound flights, and I know you have been doing that on the in-bound flights.

Could you explain to the subcommittee here exactly what we have been doing in the past and what we are doing now and why we are doing that and how it advantages us from a security risk standpoint?

Mr. WAGNER. Yes. We do get 100 percent of the commercial air and sea passengers departing the United States, their manifests in advance of departure.

Historically, we have screened them for some of our top threats that we face, terrorist screening, database hits, no-fly hits, some of our targeting and analysis hits. We have recently added the lost and stolen database query to those manifests and the screening of those manifests.

We are looking now—I want to say we get about 60 to 80 hits a day total. We are looking to program our systems to be able to see if we can administratively reconcile some of those hits so we are not chasing down, you know, some administrative-type action.

So in cases where a person hasn't updated their airline profile and the airline has transmitted the old data to us or the person has entered on a different document and we have allowed that and we can see that, we can reconcile that because they had a replacement document legitimately.

As we have seen on the in-bound, the majority of our hits are reconciled in an administrative manner because the person has a replacement document or they have lost and found their document then.

So we are seeing ways we can program our system to help us better pinpoint the ones that truly have some mollified intent and depart the United States on a true lost and stolen document.

Then we are working with TSA, also, to see if there is a way we can build in working with the airlines to put some indicators and potentially even prohibiting printing the boarding pass when we do get these hits to give us time to reconcile this information and respond.

We do rely a lot on the work the airlines and TSA already does to check the photo documentation of the traveler and ensure that traveler is properly credentialed and the work they do through the screening activities before that person does board as well, too. So we leverage a lot of those actions as well.

Mrs. MILLER. I appreciate that.

Even though we are talking about visa security and passport security, I think INTERPOL is such an interesting organization and has done just such remarkable work over the years.

You mentioned all the member countries, Mr. Bray, and the kind of information sharing you have. But let me just ask you: For instance, if you had—if somebody in Germany who was a sex offender in Germany got on an aircraft and was flying into the United States, would they be sharing that kind of information through INTERPOL with us?

I am not just talking about terrorism, but other kinds of threats to security here in the United States. Is that—just so I understand, sir, how the information sharing works through the organization.

Mr. BRAY. Yes, Madam Chairwoman. That type of information can be received, maybe—from Germany, from other countries. We routinely receive information regarding traveling sex offenders—generally, registered sex offenders in many of the countries that have a registry for that, but certainly from countries that may be just simply notifying us that a sex offender from their country is traveling.

We communicate that information immediately to our border control authorities, to CBP, so a determination can be made as to admissibility in the United States. But that is one story.

I mean, there is information regarding criminals, terrorists, modus operandi that are transmitted on a daily basis. The command center at INTERPOL Washington, as I said, is 24/7/365.

This past month they processed over 30,000 messages to and from the international law enforcement community. This is the work that we do every day. The SLTD has been just, honestly, a very key component of our work that we do and that we continue to do to enhance U.S. security.

INTERPOL Washington, as we spoke about, is a Department of Justice concern. There are no foreign law enforcement officers there.

It is strictly U.S. law enforcement, and it is us using INTERPOL and its tools to help overcome linguistic, legal, and sometimes geographic and cultural barriers that inhibit U.S. law enforcement cooperation with other foreign countries.

It has been, as you said, a great success story and it is one that I think we will be able to build upon soundly in the future.

Mrs. MILLER. Yes, Mr. Bersin.

Mr. BERSIN. The clarification—and I asked—Mr. Bray indicated that we can receive information on foreign criminal records and, in fact, the NCB is the vehicle through which 190 countries can communicate.

There are sex offender—registered sex offenders, but routinely that information actually would not come unless there is a specific case or a specific law enforcement inquiry.

Because, in fact, when a German gets on an airplane to the United States, CBP knows that he is coming, but the German authorities don't know that he is coming.

Unless that German sex offender or murderer—unless that record is in the FBI database, we have no routine insight into what is in the criminal data records of other countries.

That is the issue that—Mr. Bray is entirely right, that, if there is a specific case or a specific inquiry, NCB would receive that information.

But the point is, it is not a routine data exchange because we don't have routine access to German criminal records any more than they have routine access, unless there is a case, to our criminal records.

Mrs. MILLER. You know, one other question.

This subcommittee and our full committee is interested in pursuing some legislation in regards to biometrics for visas, et cetera, and certainly that is the only surefire way of verifying somebody's identity, I suppose, particularly for—in this case, we are only talking about foreign travelers into the United States.

Does anyone have any thoughts—again, I know we are talking about passport security, but visa security as well—in regards to how biometrics are an important tool for something like that?

Perhaps even, Ms. Sprague, from the Department of State, do you have any comment on that?

Ms. SPRAGUE. I would never pretend to be an expert on visas. But, as you know, all visa applicants do provide 10 fingerprints, and, of course, those can be verified by CBP at entry. So probably the most reliable biometric generally accepted is fingerprints, and they are already collected.

Mrs. MILLER. Anyone else have any comment on the biometrics?

Mr. BERSIN. Part of the Visa Waiver Program, Madam Chairwoman—one of the requirements Congress imposed was that we enter into something called the Preventing and Combating Serious Crime, the PCSC, agreement. There is also a national security agreement that is required that would facilitate the exchange of information.

We do have—with each of the 38 countries, we do have a PCSC agreement, and, in fact, with some countries that are not VWP members, we have those agreements. But we are just at the very dawn of creating a mechanism to exchange.

But one of the exchanges that is provided is biometric. We can query each other's fingerprint databases and then, if there is a red light or an alert, we can then follow up in the way that Ms. Sprague suggested, by having the NCB or attachés abroad say—call the police authority and say, "What is that red hit about?" and then we get the information. But we are just at the dawn of that development.

Mrs. MILLER. Well, thank you very much.

Certainly information is power. Right? Information and the sharing of information is such a critical component of our security here. So we appreciate that.

With that, the Chairwoman recognizes the Ranking Member.

Ms. JACKSON LEE. Let me thank the Chairwoman and the witnesses again.

In my opening statement, I mentioned two individuals, and I am going to mention them again because, in the present circumstances of the Malaysian Flight 370, the investigation initially has not pointed to the two individuals as having criminal intent or any intent to bring the plane down.

The initial facts—or at least what is attributed to these two individuals with false passports is a benign, but certainly important, issue of asylum and their desperation and frustration, and they might even draw empathy or sympathy.

I don't want that initial determination to cloud how serious this hearing is and how crucial it is that we have a construct that will let the world know and all the entities involved that this is a very serious issue.

I remind the witnesses, who I know already know, that Ramzi Yousef, who, in actuality, was convicted of masterminding—not just being a traveling soldier or standing by the wayside, but masterminding the 1993 World Trade Center bombing—and many who are in this business have been told and have made note of the fact that that was something that did not wake America up.

It was so unusual that we did not attribute it to a beginning change in the psyche of those who want to do America harm. But he was traveling internationally on a stolen passport.

The "White Widow," who is now wanted in Kenya, again, is linked to a fraudulent passport and a passport reported stolen. We don't know how many others.

So I think this hearing is crucial because we must leave here with the idea that solutions are possible.

I would like to, Mr. Bersin, put on the record that INTERPOL has taken note that travelers have boarded flights more than 1 billion times without having their passports checked against INTERPOL's stolen and lost travel documents. I think that is very much a wake-up call.

So I would ask you: What impediments do you think with respect to technology, infrastructure, privacy concerns are blocking or keeping countries from using the SLTD? What is your view of how the United States might be able to be helpful to these countries?

Mr. BERSIN. Thank you, Ranking Member.

You are correct with regard to the INTERPOL observation on the 1 billion——

Ms. JACKSON LEE. That is a large number.

Mr. BERSIN. A very large number, ma'am.

In your question, you indicate some of the difficulties that countries have. These include not only resource restraints in terms of lacking the money, in terms of priority of a budget decision, it also involves the lack of technological know-how and the ability to set up the kinds of sophisticated information technology systems that are required to create this kind of automated checking.

It also involves, as you indicate, the invisible requirements or constraints of privacy views and the lack of coordination between immigration authorities and police authorities at the local or provincial levels in foreign countries. All of those together create an institutional incapacity to operate the kinds of automated vetting systems that we have.

Having said that, as Mr. Wagner indicates, we have to have a strategy with regard to those countries that are critical to our security to ensure that they at the very least populate the Stolen and Lost Travel Document database. The most important requirement for us in the near term is that we actually have the data that we can vet to be able to see who may be traveling toward the United States.

The second requirement is to figure out, again, based on flows of passengers, what strategic capacity-building efforts we ought to engage in to help countries build up the kinds of technological, legal, and human capital requirements to build up these systems.

While we do that to some extent, we don't, for example, at the Department of Homeland Security have capacity-building funding, security sector assistance funding, in which to do that.

So when we go out to do that, absent a grant from the State Department or the Defense Department, we actually have to do that so-called out-of-hide, which we regularly do. But that——

Ms. JACKSON LEE. Excuse me.

But you have no budget line item that would allow you to dip into those funds and be engaged in that kind of capacity building?

Mr. BERSIN. That is correct, Ranking Member.

Ms. JACKSON LEE. So when the Secretary, Napolitano, remember, went to visit with countries dealing with TSA's responsibilities in country, meaning in foreign countries, what outreach was that?

Mr. BERSIN. So with regard to TSA, TSA, because of the responsibilities for cargo screening and airport security, has a limited separate line budget with regard to providing technical assistance on airport security. No other component to my knowledge in DHS, has a separate line item that would permit the kind of capacity building that we have talked about here this morning.

Ms. JACKSON LEE. Well, you have raised an important issue. Let me quickly pursue this very briefly, Mr. Bersin.

In your testimony, you state that despite the fact the United States has worked to incorporate recommendations for data reporting and response time in Interpol's approved standard SLTD standard operating procedure, INTERPOL does not require its member countries to implement them.

Do you have any recommendations on this and any fixes on this?

Mr. BERSIN. With regard to—as I said in response to the Chairwoman's question at the outset, Ranking Member, requiring other countries to screen the database is an open issue, in my mind, one that we need to debate, but populating the database has a direct and immediate impact on our security, so that if we go down that route, both in terms of mandates or capacity-building efforts, I would focus on getting data into the database that we could then screen as the top priority.

Whether and how we can cooperate with INTERPOL and other international organizations, such as ICAO, the International Civil Aviation Organization, is also one that we need to explore as we move forward.

Ms. JACKSON LEE. Let me quickly raise a question with Mr. Wagner and conclude with a comment. Mr. Wagner—thank you very much, Mr. Bersin.

Mr. Wagner, CBP, has long screened arriving passengers. You have not screened departing passengers. I think you started doing it after Malaysia 370.

Two questions as to why, and then Mr. Bersin said that he doesn't believe any other agency within DHS has capacity building; does your agency have that funding? I just need a yes or no on that, and then with this passport enhancing our ability to deal with fraudulent passports also help you in the human trafficking and human smuggling and human slavery issue, because I would imagine that that is also a possibility for individuals being smuggled, they may be on a fraudulent passport as well.

But the question is, you have just started doing the exiting passengers, will you continue to do it; why haven't you done it? Then what about the impact at getting our hands around stolen passports, impact on human smuggling?

Mr. WAGNER. Well, yes, we have recently added the lost and stolen documents to the outbound manifest screening that we do. We will focus primarily on before on, you know, terrorist screening database hits and other types of national security hits, but we have added those, and now we are working through to try to refine our targeting systems to help out, really to cull out some of the administrative hits that we do get——

Ms. JACKSON LEE. So will you continue?

Mr. WAGNER. Absolutely. We will be working with TSA to try to come up with a better process in that.

Ms. JACKSON LEE. Does this help you, do you believe, with issues dealing with human smuggling, human trafficking?

Mr. WAGNER. Absolutely.

Ms. JACKSON LEE. Or would it help?

Mr. WAGNER. Absolutely. Ensuring people are properly credentialed and we know who they are is a key piece of that.

As far as your capacity-building answer, I don't believe we have a specific line item for it, but we do put a lot of resources into doing that around the world or working with Department of State to be able to fund those activities.

Like I mentioned just before, that helping these governments build these types of advanced passenger information systems, to get the manifest, to get the P&R, to do the targeting and the analysis like we do, and then eventually helping exchange that information is really critical to a lot of our priorities.

Ms. JACKSON LEE. Let me just thank the Chairwoman and just say that I have questions for Ms. Sprague that I will put in the record and ask for a response for the entire committee.

Mr. Bray, I will be asking you about how you discern these resolving of possible hit, what do you do if a possible hit is discerned?

Mrs. MILLER. We will make sure the——

Ms. JACKSON LEE. We will look forward to it.

Mrs. MILLER [continuing]. Witnesses have that and——

Ms. JACKSON LEE. Thank you.

I yield back.

Mrs. MILLER [continuing]. For the committee. Thank you.

Thank the gentlelady.

Mrs. MILLER. Now the Chairwoman recognizes the gentleman from Mississippi, Mr. Palazzo.

Mr. PALAZZO. Thank you, Madam Chairwoman.

In an effort to share information related to lost and stolen passports as a criteria for participation in the visa waiver program, countries wishing to participate must sign agreements with the United States regarding the sharing of lost or stolen passports with DHS and INTERPOL. Through participation in the visa waiver program, 38 nations have agreed to share lost or stolen passport information.

Dr. Bersin, do all the visa waiver program countries routinely share information on lost or stolen passports with DHS and INTERPOL?

Mr. BERSIN. Yes, they do, Congressman Palazzo, and there is regular checking that we do to see that that requirement is met. Periodically there will be a review of how many entries have been made by visa waiver countries, and if a problem arises, we work to remedy that with a country, yes, sir.

Mr. PALAZZO. Are there any countries that are in non-compliance?

Mr. BERSIN. At this time, no. In fact, as several of us have noted in the testimony, of the 40 million records, 96 percent of them come from either visa waiver countries or E.U. countries or aspiring E.U. countries in which the requirement to populate the database is set.

Mr. PALAZZO. If a country does become in non-compliance, what actions would you take?

Mr. BERSIN. The first step would be a communication between our visa waiver program office working with components at CBP and his if necessary, to point out the deficit, and over time, we have not met this situation yet, but over time, there would be authority in the Secretary's office with Secretary Johnson to take steps to see that that effort was enforced according to the law.

Mr. PALAZZO. Okay. Because you haven't had this incidence happen yet, what would be what you think a realistic amount of time? I mean, 3 months, 6 months, dependent on the severity of the non-compliance or——

Mr. BERSIN. Because of the importance to our security vetting, we would not want that to be an extended period of time.

Mr. PALAZZO. Okay. Do you see any—I mean, I know that everybody seems to be in compliance right now, but are there any impediments or hurdles to actually providing the information that you hear from the partner nations?

Mr. BERSIN. With regard to the visa waiver nations, Congressman, as the Chairwoman pointed out at the outset, you know, these are our closest allies, these are the countries with whom we share the most experience in this area, and all of them have developed fairly sophisticated information technology systems, operating through the NCB, as Mr. Bray indicated, or independently of INTERPOL. So I think with regard to the VWP countries, we have the infrastructure in place.

Mr. PALAZZO. As a result of the requirement, do you think the sharing has been increased and do you think the program has been successful?

Mr. BERSIN. No question about that, yes.

Mr. PALAZZO. Well, thank you, Mr. Bersin.

I yield back.

Mrs. MILLER. The Chairwoman recognizes the gentleman from Texas, Mr. O'Rourke.

Mr. O'ROURKE. Thank you, Madam Chairwoman.

I appreciate you convening this hearing and so quickly exploring legislative options so soon after these vulnerabilities have been exposed, and look forward to working with you on this, and appreciate the testimony that we have heard from our experts today.

Want to thank Mr. Wagner for, and Mr. Bersin for, DHS's quick response and now querying out-bound passengers from the United States in light of the Flight 370 tragedy and everything else that you have described that we can work on, but to build upon something the Ranking Member has been asking about in terms of capacity building with other countries around the world, you responded that there is not a line item currently, but can you talk a little bit more, and perhaps starting with Mr. Bersin and then continuing with Mr. Wagner, about the wisdom of funding this capacity and efforts—in other words, providing another carrot for these other countries to participate in this?

Then my second question that you may also want to address is, in the same way that we are holding this hearing today and exploring legislative options and some of the administrative fixes that you have already put in place, maybe talk a little bit about what other countries have done over the last 3 weeks in the wake of the Flight 370 tragedy.

So, Mr. Bersin, if you would start.

Mr. BERSIN. So starting with the second question, Congressman O'Rourke, in the aftermath of the INTERPOL statements, Secretary General Ronald Noble, has been publicizing the issue, and countries around the world have taken note of the problem, and while we haven't—it is too soon to say that it has actually resulted in changes, it has created an awareness, a consciousness of the problem that simply did not exist before, and I think we will be seeing different countries within the constraints of their systems and cultures and laws taking action, and we should continue to encourage both the populating of the database, but also the screening of it.

With regard to capacity building, there are instances in which the Department of Homeland Security has received State Department grants through a variety of programs to help countries build a capacity. My point is that that is always on a grant basis and there is no long-term capacity-building line item for DHS to say, we are going to do this and encourage all of the countries in North America, from Columbia or Panama to the Arctic, to build a system so that any time someone comes into the North Americans' airspace or to a North American port, we will have insight into who is on those planes. To do that would take a large budget.

Mr. O'ROURKE. Any idea, ballpark, scope?

Mr. BERSIN. So Mr. Wagner is in a better position——

Mr. O'ROURKE. Okay.

Mr. BERSIN [continuing]. Case-by-case to give us the experience in Panama, perhaps Mexico and others, but the larger strategic vision here is that we would say over the next 10 years, while we can't build the entire panoply of measures that we have built here, we can put a minimally required and satisfactory system in place from Panama to the Arctic, working with our partner countries to do that, but that would take a budget appropriation that does not now exist.

Mr. O'ROURKE. I would think every country in the world and every person in the world who gets on an airplane has a shared interest in us resolving this, so, you know, naturally we have our allies that we have already described, the United Kingdom is already, you know, vigorously pursuing this, but we also have countries like Iran, other countries who have similar concerns about the safety and security of their citizens, and so in any way that we can provide resources or encourage others, especially wealthy countries, to share the burden to make sure everyone is participating, I would like us to explore that and would love to find either from you or from Mr. Wagner just what that cost is so that we know what we are talking about.

Mr. Wagner, do you have any thoughts on this?

Mr. WAGNER. Yeah. I don't have the cost with me today, but we did a lot of work with Mexico, Panama, and the Caribbean, too, to help these countries, with their authorities and their own internal laws and regulations, to collect airline manifest information, and then we worked with them and helped fund them in buying the systems and deploying the systems to actually go through and screen that information. We have our personnel on-site with them working with this, and then we have agreements to exchange information or take some of their information and run it through our systems and share what we can with them on that.

So there is a lot of work to do with other developing countries, and then there is also the developed world and getting a lot of our allies out there to also take like approaches to how we do this. You will find varying degrees of capacity and authorities and privacy issues with different governments doing this. We have done a lot of work with it, but really it is the consistent message that, you know, all of our allies should be doing it in a similar fashion.

Mr. O'ROURKE. As a follow-up to today's hearing, would you be able to come up with a ball-park figure and share that with the committee so that we understand, and maybe just based on, you know, past experiences with these other countries, what it would take to fund the necessary capacity globally? Not that the United States needs to bear that burden on its own, but just so that we know what that number is, and perhaps that is the basis for engaging other countries who might be able to help us to fund that, because it is in everyone's interest.

Mr. Bersin, yes.

Mr. BERSIN. Just one additional comment, and Mr. Bray can describe this in finer detail. Actually, there is an infrastructure backbone. There is one single that connects the 190 countries of INTERPOL, and it is the beginning of the kind of system that you are talking about, but perhaps Mr. Bray can explain a little more what the I–24/7 system is and why it is such a potentially important link in the area you are exploring.

Mr. O'ROURKE. Madam Chairwoman, is that all right?

Mrs. MILLER. Yes.

Mr. O'ROURKE. I am short on time.

Mrs. MILLER. I note that we have votes in about 5 minutes.

Mr. BRAY. Yes. I will be brief, sir.

Mr. O'ROURKE. Thank you.

Mr. BRAY. The I–24/7 is a backbone that connects the 190 member countries to not only INTERPOL and its resources, its databases, but to each other and directly. The ability of a country to utilize this is centered upon its National Central Bureau, so the National Central Bureau becomes a cornerstone for making sure that these utilities, these tools are made available.

With that said, the United States has been very supportive of the INTERPOL membership and the communities, specifically in Central America. We helped install sites not only at the NCB's, at specialized police units there, but also at border control points as well. We are continuing to work, as a matter of fact, prior to the airline disaster, we have been working with our counterparts in Mexico and other countries, Caribbean as well, to determine how we can better and most effectively assist them in fully realizing how those utilities and tools may be better serviced in their countries.

We will obviously work with INTERPOL to determine how we can best come up with a more global strategy for engaging countries, sharing best practices and certainly lessons learned from this process. It has been an iterative process for the United States. It has been one that has taken time to develop, and we would like to enable other countries to ramp up as quickly and efficiently as possible.

Mr. O'ROURKE. Thank you for your answer.

Thank you, Madam Chairwoman. Yield back.

Mrs. MILLER. Thank you.

Recognize the gentleman from California, Mr. Swalwell.

Mr. SWALWELL. Thank you.

Mrs. MILLER. First the Ranking Member has a comment.

Ms. JACKSON LEE. Well, I just wanted to put on the record, thank you very much for your leadership on this issue and the letter that you joined with Mr. Hudson on. This is not taking from your time, but I do appreciate. I hope that you will submit, I would like to submit your letter into the record.

Mr. SWALWELL. Yes, please.

Mrs. MILLER. Without objection.

Ms. JACKSON LEE. Dated on March 13, 2014. Again, thank you for your leadership.

Mr. SWALWELL. Thank you.

Ms. JACKSON LEE. I yield. Thank you.

[The information follows:]

LETTER SUBMITTED BY HON. SHEILA JACKSON LEE

MARCH 13, 2014.

The Honorable JEH JOHNSON,
Secretary, U.S. Department of Homeland Security, 3801 Nebraska Avenue, NW, Washington, DC 20528.

The Honorable JOHN F. KERRY,
Secretary, U.S. Department of State, 2201 C Street, NW, Washington, DC 20520.

DEAR SECRETARIES JOHNSON AND KERRY: We write with great concern regarding the security loophole highlighted by the on-going incident involving Malaysia Airlines Flight 370 ("Flight 370").

While we are still awaiting details on what happened to Flight 370 we do know that two individuals, Delavar Seyed Mohammad Reza and Pouri Nourmohammadi, were able to board an international flight carrying American passengers by using stolen passports. While these passports were in the Stolen and Lost Travel Documents (SLTD) database of INTERPOL, they were not cross referenced against it by either the airline or the appropriate authorities. This dramatically illustrates a serious flaw in airline security, one that INTERPOL has raised for years, but has not been appropriately dealt with by the international community.

While many countries, including the United States, routinely access the STLD database, many others do not. In fact, according to INTERPOL, passengers boarded airplanes more than one billion times in 2012 without having their passports screened against its databases. Allowing people to use stolen passports to travel about the world puts lives, including those of Americans, at risk.

It is imperative for passenger safety and aviation security that we close this loophole to help ensure the safety of the traveling public. Beyond assuring us, our colleagues, and the American people, that every passport used in international travel to and from the United States is always checked against the INTERPOL STLD database, we further request details on any type of program or ongoing negotiations encouraging other countries to use this database for all travelers on international flights.

While we understand that the United States is limited in its ability to alter other nation's travel and security procedures, if there are ways that Congress can get involved in encouraging responsible behavior that increases the safety of the global flying public, we hope that you will let us know.

We look forward to your prompt response. Thank you.

Sincerely,

ERIC SWALWELL,
Member of Congress.

RICHARD HUDSON,
Member of Congress.

CANDICE S. MILLER,
Member of Congress.

SHEILA JACKSON LEE,
Member of Congress.

Mrs. MILLER. The gentleman from California.

Mr. SWALWELL. Thank you to Madam Chairwoman for allowing me to participate, and thank you to the Ranking Member for supporting that request.

As others have stated, my prayers and wishes go out to the families of Malaysia Flight 370, but as we have often learned from aviation disasters, if there is any hope that has come out of it, it is that we learn a lot about our own security and how to make passenger safety much better.

I also want to note that we did, Ms. Jackson Lee and I and Chairwoman Miller and Hudson, submit a letter to the Departments of Homeland Security and State, and we both—we appreciate the swift response that we received back.

Also, I am working on legislation with Senator Schumer on the Senate side to create an incentive for countries to use this SLTD database, which is that if they don't, we simply won't issue them visas, and I hope that I can work with the Chairwoman and the Ranking Member on such legislation.

Now, Mr. Bersin, you alluded to North America as being a concern. That is my concern as well, because I believe that the countries we should principally be tracking are ones who have airports near our borders: For example, in my colleague's district, he has Juarez, Mexico, which has a large international airport; in San Diego, you have Tijuana just to the south; in Washington State, you have Vancouver airport; and of course New York, Montreal, and Toronto are not too far away.

So my first question is: To what degree are our bordering countries to the north and south, Canada and Mexico, and then of course in the hemisphere, Panama and other countries, what percentage of passengers are being screened against the database traveling in and out of those countries?

Mr. BERSIN. So with regard to Mexico, the figure, Mr. Wagner can confirm, would be 100 percent in terms of people entering Mexico. People could then cross the border and come into the United States.

With regard to Canada, the Canadians are fully cooperative with us. They screen. We are in discussions with them about the extent of the full screening. They do screen for their own citizens, and I think as a result of this incident, we will see a complete screening from our neighbors to the north.

Mr. SWALWELL. So does that mean that a flight originating in Venezuela and landing in Mexico, 100 percent of the passengers would be checked against the database on that flight?

Mr. BERSIN. That is correct. With regard to the stolen and lost travel document database, yes.

Mr. SWALWELL. Suppose a flight originating from Germany and going to Vancouver, would 100 percent be checked on that flight?

Mr. BERSIN. Yes, with regard to foreign—with regard to—against the Canadian database, yes, and against the SLTD when there is a secondary inspection, there would be a complete check. As I say, we are engaged and Canada is engaged in seeing what it can do to complete that cycle.

With regard to just your point on North America, the reason I focus on North America, presumably as you, it is not just the neighboring airports, as Juárez and El Paso, San Diego and Tijuana, Matamoros and Brownsville, but it is people coming in from outside the hemisphere into Central America, for example, then traveling overland to the border, so it is important for us to actually look at this as a continental problem, not a national one.

I think President Obama certainly in the Beyond the Border action plan with Prime Minister Harper and with Canada recognizes perimeter security as a critical issue, and I believe our Mexican colleagues and partners share this notion of perimeter security on a continental basis.

Mr. SWALWELL. Great. Thank you, Mr. Bersin.

Mr. Bray, we are beginning to learn about I–Checkit, which is a point of purchase program with INTERPOL, and what is the participation of U.S. airlines and hotels and other tourism companies right now as far as checking passports against INTERPOL's database at the point of purchase rather than 72 hours before the flight? I am just talking about the United States right now.

Mr. BRAY. With respect to the United States, I would ask Mr. Wagner. I believe that all passports are being screened, not by the airlines necessarily at the point of purchase, but certainly by CVP in the United States. Domestic purchases is what we are referring to.

Mr. SWALWELL. Right. But I–Checkit is a program intended to have cooperation with the vendors, right, the——

Mr. BRAY. Correct.

Mr. SWALWELL [continuing]. The airlines, the hotels?

Mr. BRAY. Right. So with that, the relationship, that public-private partnership relationship exists in the United States and has existed for quite some time, and as a matter of fact, it is probably a model for the world, and it is one that we have taken to INTERPOL and the I–Checkit working group. I–Checkit is currently in a very developmental stage. INTERPOL is beginning to look at how to balance the requirements and the concerns of 190 countries with a public-private partnership.

Having said that, the first models that have rolled out have been with hotels, I believe in Montenegro and Monaco, and they have seen successes there.

They are now looking specifically following the Malaysian airline disaster at the transportation sector and——

Mr. SWALWELL. But is every purchase within the United States to travel outside the United States or every purchase outside the United States to travel into the United States checked against the database at the point of purchase or is it checked closer to the departure or arrival of the flight?

Mrs. MILLER. This will be the final question.

Mr. SWALWELL. Thank you.

Mr. BRAY. It can be—they are checked when the tickets are purchased and they are also checked at the counter when they are purchased.

Mr. SWALWELL. 100 percent of the time?

Mr. BRAY. In-bound flights to the United States, yes, 100 percent of the time.

Mr. SWALWELL. Great.

Thank you, Madam Chairwoman. Yield back.

Mrs. MILLER. Thank you very much.

I certainly want to thank the witnesses for all being here today. Obviously the Members, I think almost all of us, have additional questions, so I would invite you all, of course, to submit those for the witnesses, and we will ask for a written response to the questions.

Again, I appreciate you coming really on pretty short notice. We convened this hearing, I had an idea to do it and convened it pretty quickly, particularly for how things move here around Capitol Hill, so we appreciate all the witnesses coming this morning.

Pursuant to the Committee Rule 7(e), the hearing record will be held open for 10 days.

Without objection, the committee now stands adjourned.

Thanks again.

[Whereupon, at 10:25 a.m., the subcommittee was adjourned.]

APPENDIX

QUESTIONS FROM HONORABLE ERIC SWALWELL FOR ALAN D. BERSIN

Question 1. Assistant Secretary Bersin, with respect to Canada, you appeared to testify that right now Canada only screens its own citizens going to and from Canada on international travel against the Stolen and Lost Travel Documents (SLTD) database on a routine basis. Is that correct? What percentage of all passengers flying to Canada are checked against SLTD database by Canada? What percentage of all passengers leaving Canada by air are checked against the SLTD database by Canada?

Answer. To clarify, presently Canada screens all travelers' documents against a Canadian database of lost/stolen/fraudulent documents when they enter Canada. Canada's database is comprised of data from Passport Canada, Citizenship and Immigration Canada, and provincial authorities, and also includes data provided by foreign authorities and Canadian overseas liaison officers. Currently, Canada does not screen travelers against the INTERPOL SLTD database during primary inspection, but Canadian officers at secondary inspection can access the SLTD database and query it when necessary. At present, Canada does not systematically screen out-bound travelers against its database of lost/stolen/fraudulent documents, but will have the capability to do so with the implementation of Interactive Advance Passenger Data and Entry/Exit in the air mode.

Question 2. You also suggested Canada is moving toward 100 percent international air passenger screening against the SLTD database. What work is the United States doing to help encourage Canada to get to 100 percent screening? Would this include in-bound and out-bound passengers traveling by air? What is your understanding of Canada's current plan to reach this goal? When will Canada reach it?

Answer. Canada has not yet formally committed to 100 percent international air passenger screening against the SLTD database. DHS has, however, begun initial outreach to our Canadian counterparts to discuss this matter and share related best practices that the United States has adopted.

Question 3. Besides Canada and Mexico, which countries in North America and Central America, if any, check travel documents of 100 percent of international travelers entering their country by air travel against the INTERPOL SLTD database? Which check 100 percent of such air travelers leaving the country?

Answer. DHS can confirm that the travel documents of all international travelers entering the following countries are checked against the SLTD database: Antigua and Barbuda; Barbados; Dominica; Grenada; Guyana; Jamaica; Mexico; Panama; St. Kitts and Nevis; Saint Lucia; St. Vincent and the Grenadines; and Trinidad and Tobago.

Unfortunately DHS does not have detailed information regarding the specific screening practices of all INTERPOL member countries, including whether they screen against the SLTD database. However, INTERPOL Washington is best positioned to be able to assist in gathering this information from the INTERPOL General Secretariat.

Question 4. In your prepared testimony you note that "many countries do not have advance passenger information capabilities to screen travelers prior to arrival." Is this lack of infrastructure the most significant impediment to use of the STLD database? If not, what is? If so, how can the United States help address that problem? What else should the United States be doing to encourage countries to scan international air passengers against the SLTD database?

Answer. Many countries lack an advance passenger information system and the required infrastructure, which significantly hinders their ability to screen in-bound air passengers against the SLTD database prior to their arrival. The United States can help address this problem through capacity-building efforts and the promotion of international security standards. Moreover, the United States can strongly encourage countries to routinely report lost and stolen passport data to INTERPOL for inclusion into the SLTD database. DHS screens every person seeking admission into the United States (whether by air, land, or sea) against the SLTD database, so prompting countries that do not currently report lost and stolen passport data to do so is critical.

Question 5. In your prepared testimony you mention that one way the Department of Homeland Security (DHS) is helping encourage countries to use the SLTD database is through the establishment of the Integrated Border Management Task Force (IBMTF). Beyond training officials, what is the IBMTF doing to promote the use of SLTD? What else is DHS doing in this regard?

Answer. The IBMTF primarily conducts training operations for border management and law enforcement officials regarding utilizing INTERPOL tools that are available to them. For example, as part of a 2-week program, INTERPOL officials will bring mobile devices to an international airport, so that immigration officers can check passports against the SLTD and INTERPOL's other datasets. These programs often yield positive results including the arrest of wanted persons or the denied entry of suspected criminals. DHS is committed to helping INTERPOL build and operate the IBMTF, by offering expertise and best practices in border management.

As part of the biennial reviews of VWP countries, DHS evaluates the effectiveness of their border screening procedures and immigration controls. Among other things, DHS verifies that VWP countries report lost and stolen passports to INTERPOL, as required by the VWP statute. DHS also used the biennial reviews to encourage the border control authorities in VWP countries to search the SLTD database in the screening of all international travelers.

Question 6. Beyond its participation in IBMTF, what specific actions has DHS undertaken in the past to encourage other countries to use the SLTD database for international air travel? What specific actions are planned by DHS to do this in the future?

Answer. At numerous INTERPOL events and conferences, DHS senior leadership has encouraged INTERPOL member countries to use the SLTD database to enhance security across the global travel continuum. Looking ahead, DHS plans to engage partner countries bilaterally and through multilateral fora to further encourage them to report data into the SLTD database and to adopt enhanced screening procedures.

QUESTIONS FROM HONORABLE ERIC SWALWELL FOR JACK P. WAGNER

Question 1. Assistant Commissioner Wagner, I sent a letter to Department of Homeland Security (DHS) Secretary Jeh Johnson, asking in part about U.S. screening practices. From the response I received from DHS, I take it that every single traveler coming into the United States is checked against the INTERPOL Stolen and Lost Travel Documents (SLTD) database. I want to understand more about the process.

How much time before a flight is scheduled to take off does U.S. Customs and Border Protection (CBP) receive information about passenger lists to be able to screen against the SLTD database?

Question 2. When, after CBP receives information about passengers, does it begin screening against the SLTD database? When does it finish the check?

Question 3. According to your testimony, if a hit is found and an airline boards the passenger regardless, the airline can be fined. Can CBP do anything else to prevent the plane from landing in the United States? Or, can it act to prevent the passenger in question from disembarking if the plane does come here with that passenger?

Question 4. I understand what happens if CBP finds a hit in its screening. But, what happens if the screening is not completed before the scheduled take-off?

Answer. The Intelligence Reform and Terrorism Prevention Act (IRTPA) of 2004 required the Federal Government where practicable to conduct Terrorist Watch List screening prior to departure. To meet IRTPA requirements, U.S. Customs and Border Protection (CBP) modified the Advance Passenger Information System (APIS) and developed interactive communications to provide carriers with real-time terrorist watch list screening results. CBP now starts receiving available APIS data from airlines 72 hours prior to departure and, under 19 CFR 122.49a and 122.75a, airlines must transmit all passenger data no later than the time of securing the aircraft doors for departure.

Passenger data that contains a passport number is immediately screened against the SLTD upon receipt. Any re-submission of passport data prompts a re-screening through the SLTD. The initial check is completed electronically in a matter of seconds and a new query is executed each time passport data is submitted.

CBP has the authority per 19 CFR 122.14(d) to revoke landing rights of a carrier, though this should not be invoked absent exigent circumstances. CBP has a "detain on-board" process for vessels but not for aircraft since, in many cases, the aircraft might not immediately return to its destination or the aircraft may fly on to another location. In these cases the traveler would be detained at the port of entry for processing and, if they are found inadmissible, the airline would return the traveler on the next flight to the point of embarkation.

The SLTD query is designed to repeat until results are received. If a response to a SLTD query is not received electronically within 7 minutes, the query is considered "timed out" and a new query is executed. If results were received after departure, (for example, if the INTERPOL SLTD connection was down for a significant amount of time), the hit would be displayed for CBP officers at the port of entry and adjudicated at the time of arrival.

QUESTIONS FROM HONORABLE ERIC SWALWELL FOR BRENDA S. SPRAGUE

Question 1a. What specific actions has the State Department taken to encourage other countries to check passports by travelers used in international flights against the SLTD database, as opposed to merely share data with INTERPOL?

Answer. On April 18, the Department of State, on behalf of the Department of Homeland Security, reached out to INTERPOL member countries to gather information about their practices related to the access and use of the Stolen and Lost Travel Document Database (SLTD). We also used this as an opportunity to remind member countries of the importance to both input their lost/stolen data into the SLTD and to use the SLTD when screening travelers. A survey targeting specific usage practices has been forwarded to INTERPOL members to solicit how and under what circumstances border control officials utilize the SLTD. The results of this survey will help the State Department tailor our efforts to encourage elimination of weaknesses or inconsistencies in the usage and access of the SLTD.

Question 1b. In light of the Malaysia Air incident, what specific steps does the State Department plan to further encourage countries to check the passports of passengers in international flights against the SLTD database?

Answer. The goal of sharing lost and stolen passport data with governments has been endorsed repeatedly as an international objective, including through the International Civil Aviation Organization (ICAO), European Union, Organization for Security and Cooperation in Europe, and G–8 processes. The Department of State is active and engaged with each of these multilateral organizations. We continue to support international efforts and encourage all governments to share and use this vital information.

We believe that the best way to encourage other countries to check the passports of all passengers on international flights against the SLTD database is through an active engagement with the ICAO. The next opportunity for discussions on this issue is at the next ICAO Technical Advisory Group on Machine Readable Travel Documents Meeting on May 21 in Montreal, Canada.

Question 2a. I want to ask about reasons the SLTD database may not be used. The State Department automatically screens visa applicants against the INTERPOL database. Does it find this to be burdensome or otherwise difficult?

Answer. Visa processing posts see an average of only around 90 applications per month world-wide with passport hits from the Stolen and Lost Travel Document (STLD) database. This is a small fraction of the visa workload, considering that the Department has over 220 overseas posts that processed more than 11.5 million visa transactions in fiscal year 2013.

Consular officers are required to definitively resolve all hits returned by SLTD checks before issuing visas. In the majority of cases involving visa applicants with SLTD hits, posts found that passports were reported as lost or stolen when they were misplaced by holders who later recovered them, or lost or stolen passports were listed on the visa application, but applicants presented a new passport in support of the application.

While the number of visa applicant passport hits in the SLTD is small, the State Department finds that the process and the investment in information technology to establish the capability to conduct clearances against the SLTD is not unduly burdensome, given the potential to deter mala fide travelers.

Question 2b. What problems have other countries cited to the State Department for not checking passports against the SLTD database? Do you think these problems are legitimate or are they just excuses for not having the will or desire to follow

through? If the problems are legitimate, what can and should the United States do
to assist?

Answer. The Department of State believes that accurate answers to these two
questions can only come from INTERPOL—the organization charged with operating
the SLTD. However, in the Department of State's interactions on this and other
similar issues, many countries voice concerns about resources and available technological infrastructure. Weak governance structures might also impede the development of improved reporting mechanisms within some member countries.

QUESTIONS FROM HONORABLE ERIC SWALWELL FOR SHAWN BRAY

Question 1. Do you believe checking passports at the point of purchase would be
an improvement over our current system? Why or why not?

Answer. Unless the process remained inherently governmental, INTERPOL
Washington would not recommend this course of action. Point-of-purchase sales,
particularly for airlines, can occur as far as a year in advance. The overwhelming
majority of SLTD hits are administrative in nature as opposed to involving persons
committing criminal acts. Of these hits, most fall into two main categories: Individuals traveling on passports previously issued to them but reported as lost or stolen,
and individuals using travel agencies or automated systems, and whose stored passport information has not been changed since the document was reported lost or stolen. Point-of-purchase sales, particularly for airlines, can occur as far as a year in
advance. Transactions made months or days in advance will therefore continue to
generate administrative hits, creating additional resource strains on border and law
enforcement officials.

On the other hand, if airlines or cruise lines were made directly aware that a
passport used to make a reservation was not valid, they could reconcile the issue
with the traveler without the need for law enforcement intervention. The number
of administrative hits would be thereby greatly reduced, allowing law enforcement
authorities to concentrate on unresolved SLTD hits, including those that are potentially criminal in nature. The guidelines for how this process would work would
need to be clearly defined.

Question 2. What is the status of the I–Checkit system? What is your projection
for when it will be widely available? What impediments are there to its development
and use?

Answer. INTERPOL's I–Checkit Program is still in the developmental stage. An
initial, small-scale pilot of the program has been scheduled for some time in late
2014 or early 2015. A time line for full implementation has yet to be announced.

While I–Checkit is meant to encompass a variety of areas, it is presently focused
on the transportation sector. Impediments largely stem from differences in national
legislation and policies among the INTERPOL member countries and primarily include privacy issues surrounding the use of travel document data and the direct engagement with private-sector partners by INTERPOL.

Question 3. Which countries rarely, if ever, screen international passenger against
the INTERPOL SLTD database?

Answer. In 2013, approximately 91 percent of all queries made against
INTERPOL's SLTD database by INTERPOL member countries were made by the
United States, United Kingdom, United Arab Emirates, and Japan. While many of
the 167 signatory countries and international organizations participating in the program search the database on a regular basis, the majority of them do not use the
database to screen international passengers; however, they do use it for investigative purposes.

Question 4. With respect to countries in North America and Central America,
when, if ever, are travel documents checked for 100 percent of international travelers entering by air travel against the INTERPOL SLTD database? For which
countries are 100 percent of such air travelers leaving the country checked?

Answer. The United States is currently the only country known to perform SLTD
checks on 100 percent of all passengers traveling in-bound or out-bound by air.

Question 5. What percentage of the times when international air travelers are
screened against the INTERPOL SLTD database is a hit found which suggests possible criminal theft?

Answer. On average, only a handful of SLTD hits are the result of a criminal act.
The exact number is hard to obtain since many countries do not report the final
disposition of SLTD hits that occur in their countries. INTERPOL Washington is
currently proposing INTERPOL require greater visibility and accountability by its
member countries for the final disposition of all SLTD hits.

Question 6a. Which of these reasons (national policy; lack of connection or cooperation between law enforcement, issuing, and border control authorities; and ca-

pacity, i.e. cost of deployment and existing infrastructure) is the primary one for why countries do not screen international air travelers against the SLTD database?

Answer. The reasons for not screening international air travelers against the SLTD database vary from country to country. For some, particularly underdeveloped countries, the lack of an adequate information technology (IT) infrastructure creates communication and capacity issues that hamper implementation of the system. Other factors that have been cited include cost, national policy, privacy concerns, and various bureaucratic obstacles—regardless of the state of the country's IT infrastructure. Any combination of these factors makes this problem correspondingly more complex and challenging to address.

It should also be noted that merely being connected to the database does not optimize its use in screening international air travelers. The timely resolution of hits against the database is also indispensable in preventing potentially illicit travel. For some countries with limited law enforcement and border control assets and capabilities, this presents a particularly difficult and continuing challenge.

It's important that the United States work closely with INTERPOL and its member countries to share best practices and determine where we might be able to assist in capacity building. To that end, INTERPOL Washington is currently working with the Department of Homeland Security (DHS) and the Department of State (DoS) on a global initiative to gain a better understanding of the obstacles impeding other countries' ability to use the SLTD database on a consistent and regular basis.

Question 6b. What can the United States do to help countries address this primary reason? What can we do to address any of the other obstacles?

Answer. Supported by the Department of Justice and DHS, INTERPOL Washington is partnering with DoS to establish a whole-of-government approach to encourage those foreign ministries responsible for the issuance of travel documents to work with INTERPOL and their respective National Central Bureaus (NCB) to improve cooperation and fully participate in the SLTD program. Regionally speaking, INTERPOL Washington is working with personnel from the U.S. Embassy in Mexico City, the government of Mexico, and NCB Mexico City to identify the specific issues that impact them and neighboring countries from fully participating in the SLTD program. Once clearly identified, INTERPOL Washington intends to seek support for the requisite technical and diplomatic assistance. The results of this initiative will then be used as an example of best practices that could be adopted globally.

Additionally, we are encouraging the INTERPOL General Secretariat in Lyon, France to enhance the management and oversight of the SLTD Program in order to foster improvements that would ensure SLTD and its technology remains current and increases the ease of access and use by more INTERPOL member countries. Our leadership and efforts to improve the SLTD program were recently recognized when INTERPOL Washington was voted to chair INTERPOL's multi-national SLTD Advisory Committee in Lyon, France. This leadership position on the advisory committee will provide the United States with a unique platform to share best practices, influence policy, and help guide operations pertaining to INTERPOL's SLTD program.

○